CLEP-41   COLLEGE-LEVEL EXAMINATION
PROGRAM SERIES

*This is your
PASSBOOK for...*

# Principles of/ Introductory Macroeconomics

*Test Preparation Study Guide
Questions & Answers*

# COPYRIGHT NOTICE

This book is SOLELY intended for, is sold ONLY to, and its use is RESTRICTED to individual, bona fide applicants or candidates who qualify by virtue of having seriously filed applications for appropriate license, certificate, professional and/or promotional advancement, higher school matriculation, scholarship, or other legitimate requirements of education and/or governmental authorities.

This book is NOT intended for use, class instruction, tutoring, training, duplication, copying, reprinting, excerption, or adaptation, etc., by:

1) Other publishers
2) Proprietors and/or Instructors of "Coaching" and/or Preparatory Courses
3) Personnel and/or Training Divisions of commercial, industrial, and governmental organizations
4) Schools, colleges, or universities and/or their departments and staffs, including teachers and other personnel
5) Testing Agencies or Bureaus
6) Study groups which seek by the purchase of a single volume to copy and/or duplicate and/or adapt this material for use by the group as a whole without having purchased individual volumes for each of the members of the group
7) Et al.

Such persons would be in violation of appropriate Federal and State statutes.

PROVISION OF LICENSING AGREEMENTS – Recognized educational, commercial, industrial, and governmental institutions and organizations, and others legitimately engaged in educational pursuits, including training, testing, and measurement activities, may address request for a licensing agreement to the copyright owners, who will determine whether, and under what conditions, including fees and charges, the materials in this book may be used them. In other words, a licensing facility exists for the legitimate use of the material in this book on other than an individual basis. However, it is asseverated and affirmed here that the material in this book CANNOT be used without the receipt of the express permission of such a licensing agreement from the Publishers. Inquiries re licensing should be addressed to the company, attention rights and permissions department.

All rights reserved, including the right of reproduction in whole or in part, in any form or by any means, electronic or mechanical, including photocopying, recording, or by any information storage and retrieval system, without permission in writing from the Publisher.

Copyright © 2025 by
## National Learning Corporation

212 Michael Drive, Syosset, NY 11791
(516) 921-8888 • www.passbooks.com
E-mail: info@passbooks.com

# PASSBOOK® SERIES

THE *PASSBOOK® SERIES* has been created to prepare applicants and candidates for the ultimate academic battlefield – the examination room.

At some time in our lives, each and every one of us may be required to take an examination – for validation, matriculation, admission, qualification, registration, certification, or licensure.

Based on the assumption that every applicant or candidate has met the basic formal educational standards, has taken the required number of courses, and read the necessary texts, the *PASSBOOK® SERIES* furnishes the one special preparation which may assure passing with confidence, instead of failing with insecurity. Examination questions – together with answers – are furnished as the basic vehicle for study so that the mysteries of the examination and its compounding difficulties may be eliminated or diminished by a sure method.

This book is meant to help you pass your examination provided that you qualify and are serious in your objective.

The entire field is reviewed through the huge store of content information which is succinctly presented through a provocative and challenging approach – the question-and-answer method.

A climate of success is established by furnishing the correct answers at the end of each test.

You soon learn to recognize types of questions, forms of questions, and patterns of questioning. You may even begin to anticipate expected outcomes.

You perceive that many questions are repeated or adapted so that you can gain acute insights, which may enable you to score many sure points.

You learn how to confront new questions, or types of questions, and to attack them confidently and work out the correct answers.

You note objectives and emphases, and recognize pitfalls and dangers, so that you may make positive educational adjustments.

Moreover, you are kept fully informed in relation to new concepts, methods, practices, and directions in the field.

You discover that you are actually taking the examination all the time: you are preparing for the examination by "taking" an examination, not by reading extraneous and/or supererogatory textbooks.

In short, this PASSBOOK®, used directedly, should be an important factor in helping you to pass your test.

# NONTRADITIONAL EDUCATION

Students returning to school as adults bring more varied experience to their studies than do the teenagers who begin college shortly after graduating from high school. As a result, there are numerous programs for students with nontraditional learning curves. Hundreds of colleges and universities grant degrees to people who cannot attend classes at a regular campus or have already learned what the college is supposed to teach.

You can earn nontraditional education credits in many ways:
- Passing standardized exams
- Demonstrating knowledge gained through experience
- Completing campus-based coursework, and
- Taking courses off campus

Some methods of assessing learning for credit are objective, such as standardized tests. Others are more subjective, such as a review of life experiences.

With some help from four hypothetical characters – Alice, Vin, Lynette, and Jorge – this article describes nontraditional ways of earning educational credit. It begins by describing programs in which you can earn a high school diploma without spending 4 years in a classroom. The college picture is more complicated, so it is presented in two parts: one on gaining credit for what you know through course work or experience, and a second on college degree programs. The final section lists resources for locating more information.

## Earning High School Credit

People who were prevented from finishing high school as teenagers have several options if they want to do so as adults. Some major cities have back-to-school programs that allow adults to attend high school classes with current students. But the more practical alternatives for most adults are to take the General Educational Development (GED) tests or to earn a high school diploma by demonstrating their skills or taking correspondence classes.

Of course, these options do not match the experience of staying in high school and graduating with one's friends. But they are viable alternatives for adult learners committed to meeting and, often, continuing their educational goals.

### GED Program

Alice quit high school her sophomore year and took a job to help support herself, her younger brother, and their newly widowed mother. Now an adult, she wants to earn her high school diploma – and then go on to college. Because her job as head cook and her family responsibilities keep her busy during the day, she plans to get a high school equivalency diploma. She will study for, and take, the GED tests. Every year, about half a million adults earn their high school credentials this way. A GED diploma is accepted in lieu of a high school one by more than 90 percent of employers, colleges, and universities, so it is a good choice for someone like Alice.

The GED testing program is sponsored by the American Council on Education and State and local education departments. It consists of examinations in five subject areas: Writing, science, mathematics, social studies, and literature and the arts. The tests also measure skills such as analytical ability, problem solving, reading comprehension, and ability to understand and apply information. Most of the questions are multiple choice; the writing test includes an essay section on a topic of general interest.

Eligibility rules for taking the exams vary, but some states require that you must be at least 18. Tests are given in English, Spanish, and French. In addition to standard print, versions in large print, Braille, and audiocassette are also available. Total time allotted for the tests is 7 1/2 hours.

The GED tests are not easy. About one-fourth of those who complete the exams every year do not pass. Passing scores are established by administering the tests to a sample of graduating high school seniors. The minimum standard score is set so that about one-third of graduating seniors would not pass the tests if they took them.

Because of the difficulty of the tests, people need to prepare themselves to take them. Often, they start by taking the Official GED Practice Tests, usually available through a local adult education center. Centers are listed in your phone book's blue pages under "Adult Education," "Continuing Education," or "GED." Adult education centers also have information about GED preparation classes and self-study materials. Classes are generally arranged to accommodate adults' work schedules. National Learning Corporation publishes several study guides that aim to thoroughly prepare test-takers for the GED.

School districts, colleges, adult education centers, and community organizations have information about GED testing schedules and practice tests. For more information, contact them, your nearest GED testing center, or:

GED Testing Service
One Dupont Circle, NW, Suite 250
Washington, DC 20036-1163
1(800) 62-MY GED (626-9433)
(202) 939-9490

**Skills Demonstration**

Adults who have acquired high school level skills through experience might be eligible for the National External Diploma Program. This alternative to the GED does not involve any direct instruction. Instead, adults seeking a high school diploma must demonstrate mastery of 65 competencies in 8 general areas: Communication; computation; occupational preparedness; and self, social, consumer, scientific, and technological awareness.

Mastery is shown through the completion of the tasks. For example, a participant could prove competency in computation by measuring a room for carpeting, figuring out the amount of carpet needed, and computing the cost.

Before being accepted for the program, adults undergo an evaluation. Tests taken at one of the program's offices measure reading, writing, and mathematics abilities. A take-home segment includes a self-assessment of current skills, an individual skill evaluation, and an occupational interest and aptitude test.

Adults accepted for the program have weekly meetings with an assessor. At the meeting, the assessor reviews the participant's work from the previous week. If the task has not been completed properly, the assessor explains the mistake. Participants continue to correct their errors until they master each competency. A high school diploma is awarded upon proven mastery of all 65 competencies.

Fourteen States and the District of Columbia now offer the External Diploma Program. For more information, contact:

External Diploma Program
One Dupont Circle, NW, Suite 250
Washington, DC 20036-1193
(202) 939-9475

**Correspondence and Distance Study**

Vin dropped out of high school during his junior year because his family's frequent moves made it difficult for him to continue his studies. He promised himself at the time he dropped out that he would someday finish the courses needed for his diploma. For people like Vin, who prefer to earn a traditional diploma in a nontraditional way, there are about a dozen accredited courses of study for earning a high school diploma by correspondence, or distance study. The programs are either privately run, affiliated with a university, or administered by a State education department.

Distance study diploma programs have no residency requirements, allowing students to continue their studies from almost any location. Depending on the course of study, students need not be enrolled full time and usually have more flexible schedules for finishing their work. Selection of courses ranges from vo-tech to college prep, and some programs place different emphasis on the types of diplomas offered. University affiliated schools, for example, allow qualified students to take college courses along with their high school ones. Students can then apply the college credits toward a degree at that university or transfer them to another institution.

Taking courses by distance study is often more challenging and time consuming than attending classes, especially for adults who have other obligations. Success depends on each student's motivation. Students usually do reading assignments on their own. Written exercises, which they complete and send to an instructor for grading, supplement their reading material.

A list of some accredited high schools that offer diplomas by distance study is available free from the Distance Education and Training Council, formerly known as the National Home Study Council. Request the "DETC Directory of Accredited Institutions" from:

The Distance Education and Training Council
1601 18th Street, NW.
Washington, DC 20009-2529
(202) 234-5100

Some publications profiling nontraditional college programs include addresses and descriptions of several high school correspondence ones. See the Resources section at the end of this article for more information.

**Getting College Credit For What You Know**

Adults can receive college credit for prior coursework, by passing examinations, and documenting experiential learning. With help from a college advisor, nontraditional students should assess their skills, establish their educational goals, and determine the number of college credits they might be eligible for.

Even before you meet with a college advisor, you should collect all your school and training records. Then, make a list of all knowledge and abilities acquired through experience, no matter how irrelevant they seem to your chosen field.  Next, determine your educational goals:  What specific field do you wish to study?  What kind of a degree do you want?  Finally, determine how your past work fits into the field of study.  Later on, you will evaluate educational programs to find one that's right for you.

People who have complex educational or experiential learning histories might want to have their learning evaluated by the Regents Credit Bank.  The Credit Bank, operated by Regents College of the University of the State of New York, allows people to consolidate credits earned through college, experience, or other methods.  Special assessments are available for Regents College enrollees whose knowledge in a specific field cannot be adequately evaluated by standardized exams.  For more information, contact the Regents Credit Bank at:

Regents College
7 Columbia Circle
Albany, NY 12203-5159
(518) 464-8500

**Credit For Prior College Coursework**

When Lynette was in college during the 1970s, she attended several different schools and took a variety of courses.  She did well in some classes and poorly in others.  Now that she is a successful business owner and has more focus, Lynette thinks she should forget about her previous coursework and start from scratch.  Instead, she should start from where she is.

Lynette should have all her transcripts sent to the colleges or universities of her choice and let an admissions officer determine which classes are applicable toward a degree.  A few credits here and there may not seem like much, but they add up.  Even if the subjects do not seem relevant to any major, they might be counted as elective credits toward a degree.  And comparing the cost of transcripts with the cost of college courses, it makes sense to spend a few dollars per transcript for a chance to save hundreds, and perhaps thousands, of dollars in books and tuition.

Rules for transferring credits apply to all prior coursework at accredited colleges and universities, whether done on campus or off.  Courses completed off campus, often called extended learning, include those available to students through independent study and correspondence.  Many schools have extended learning programs; Brigham Young University, for example, offers more than 300 courses through its Department of Independent Study.  One type of extended learning is distance learning, a form of correspondence study by technological means such as television, video and audio, CD-ROM, electronic mail, and computer tutorials.  See the Resources section at the end of this article for more information about publications available from the National University Continuing Education Association.

Any previously earned college credits should be considered for transfer, no matter what the subject or the grade received.  Many schools do not accept the transfer of courses graded below a C or ones taken more than a designated number of years ago.  Some colleges and universities also have limits on the number of credits that can be transferred and applied toward a degree.  But not all do.  For example, Thomas Edison State College, New Jersey's State college for adults, accepts the transfer of all 120 hours of credit required for a baccalaureate degree – provided all the credits are transferred from regionally accredited schools, no more than 80 are at the junior college level, and the student's grades overall and in the field of study average out to C.

To assign credit for prior coursework, most schools require original transcripts. This means you must complete a form or send a written, signed request to have your transcripts released directly to a college or university. Once you have chosen the schools you want to apply to, contact the schools you attended before. Find out how much each transcript costs, and ask them to send your transcripts to the ones you are applying to. Write a letter that includes your name (and names used during attendance, if different) and dates of attendance, along with the names and addresses of the schools to which your transcripts should be sent. Include payment and mail to the registrar at the schools you have attended. The registrar's office will process your request and send an official transcript of your coursework to the colleges or universities you have designated.

**Credit For Noncollege Courses**

Colleges and universities are not the only ones that offer classes. Volunteer organizations and employers often provide formal training worth college credit. The American Council on Education has two programs that assess thousands of specific courses and make recommendations on the amount of college credit they are worth. Colleges and universities accept the recommendations or use them as guidelines.

One program evaluates educational courses sponsored by government agencies, business and industry, labor unions, and professional and voluntary organizations. It is the Program on Noncollegiate Sponsored Instruction (PONSI). Some of the training seminars Alice has participated in covered topics such as food preparation, kitchen safety, and nutrition. Although she has not yet earned her GED, Alice can earn college credit because of her completion of these formal job-training seminars. The number of credits each seminar is worth does not hinge on Alice's current eligibility for college enrollment.

The other program evaluates courses offered by the Army, Navy, Air Force, Marines, Coast Guard, and Department of Defense. It is the Military Evaluations Program. Jorge has never attended college, but the engineering technology classes he completed as part of his military training are worth college credit. And as an Army veteran, Jorge is eligible for a service that takes the evaluations one step further. The Army/American Council on Education Registry Transcript System (AARTS) will provide Jorge with an individualized transcript of American Council on Education credit recommendations for all courses he completed, the military occupational specialties (MOS's) he held, and examinations he passed while in the Army. All Army and National Guard enlisted personnel and veterans who enlisted after October 1981 are eligible for the transcript. Similar services are being considered by the Navy and Marine Corps.

To obtain a free transcript, see your Army Education Center for a 5454R transcript request form. Include your name, Social Security number, basic active service date, and complete address where you want the transcript sent. Mail your request to:
AARTS Operations Center
415 McPherson Ave.
Fort Leavenworth, KS 66027-1373

Recommendations for PONSI are published in *The National Guide to Educational Credit for Training Programs;* military program recommendations are in *The Guide to the Evaluation of Educational Experiences in the Armed Forces.* See the Resources section at the end of this article for more information about these publications.

Former military personnel who took a foreign language course through the Defense Language Institute may request course transcripts by sending their name, Social Security number, course title, duration of the course, and graduation date to:

> Commandant, Defense Language Institute
> Attn: ATFL-DAA-AR
> Transcripts
> Presidio of Monterey
> Monterey, CA 93944-5006

Not all of Jorge's and Alice's courses have been assessed by the American Council on Education. Training courses that have no Council credit recommendation should still be assessed by an advisor at the schools they want to attend. Course descriptions, class notes, test scores, and other documentation may be helpful for comparing training courses to their college equivalents. An oral examination or other demonstration of competency might also be required.

There is no guarantee you will receive all the credits you are seeking – but you certainly won't if you make no attempt.

**Credit By Examination**

Standardized tests are the best-known method of receiving college credit without taking courses. These exams are often taken by high school students seeking advanced placement for college, but they are also available to adult learners. Testing programs and colleges and universities offer exams in a number of subjects. Two U.S. Government institutes have foreign language exams for employees that also may be worth college credit.

It is important to understand that receiving a passing score on these exams does not mean you get college credit automatically. Each school determines which test results it will accept, minimum scores required, how scores are converted for credit, and the amount of credit, if any, to be assigned. Most colleges and universities accept the American Council on Education credit recommendations, published every other year in the 250-page *Guide to Educational Credit by Examination*. For more information, contact:

> The American Council on Education
> Credit by Examination Program
> One Dupont Circle, Suite 250
> Washington, DC 20036-1193
> (202) 939-9434

*Testing programs:*

You might know some of the five national testing programs by their acronyms or initials: CLEP, ACT PEP: RCE, DANTES, AP, and NOCTI. (The meanings of these initialisms are explained below.) There is some overlap among programs; for example, four of them have introductory accounting exams. Since you will not be awarded credit more than once for a specific subject, you should carefully evaluate each program for the subject exams you wish to take. And before taking an exam, make sure you will be awarded credit by the college or university you plan to attend.

CLEP (College-Level Examination Program), administered by the College Board, is the most widely accepted of the national testing programs; more than 2,800 accredited schools award credit for passing exam scores. Each test covers material taught in basic undergraduate courses. There are five general exams – English composition, humanities, college mathematics, natural sciences, and social sciences and history – and many subject exams. Most exams are entirely multiple-choice, but English composition exams may include an essay section. For more information, contact:

    CLEP
    P.O. Box 6600
    Princeton, NJ 08541-6600
    (609) 771-7865

ACT PEP: RCE (American College Testing Proficiency Exam Program: Regents College Examinations) tests are given in 38 subjects within arts and sciences, business, education, and nursing. Each exam is recommended for either lower- or upper-level credit. Exams contain either objective or extended response questions, and are graded according to a standard score, letter grade, or pass/fail. Fees vary, depending on the subject and type of exam. For more information or to request free study guides, contact:

    ACT PEP: Regents College Examinations
    P.O. Box 4014
    Iowa City, IA 52243
    (319) 337-1387
    (New York State residents must contact Regents College directly.)

DANTES (Defense Activity for Nontraditional Education Support) standardized tests are developed by the Educational Testing Service for the Department of Defense. Originally administered only to military personnel, the exams have been available to the public since 1983. About 50 subject tests cover business, mathematics, social science, physical science, humanities, foreign languages, and applied technology. Most of the tests consist entirely of multiple-choice questions. Schools determine their own administering fees and testing schedules. For more information or to request free study sheets, contact:

    DANTES Program Office
    Mail Stop 31-X
    Educational Testing Service
    Princeton, NJ 08541
    1(800) 257-9484

The AP (Advanced Placement) Program is a cooperative effort between secondary schools and colleges and universities. AP exams are developed each year by committees of college and high school faculty appointed by the College Board and assisted by consultants from the Educational Testing Service. Subjects include arts and languages, natural sciences, computer science, social sciences, history, and mathematics. Most tests are 2 or 3 hours long and include both multiple-choice and essay questions. AP courses are available to help students prepare for exams, which are offered in the spring. For more information about the Advanced Placement Program, contact:

    Advanced Placement Services
    P.O. Box 6671
    Princeton, NJ 08541-6671
    (609) 771-7300

NOCTI (National Occupational Competency Testing Institute) assessments are designed for people like Alice, who have vocational-technical skills that cannot be evaluated by other tests. NOCTI assesses competency at two levels: Student/job ready and teacher/experienced worker. Standardized evaluations are available for occupations such as auto-body repair, electronics, mechanical drafting, quantity food preparation, and upholstering. The tests consist of multiple-choice questions and a performance component. Other services include workshops, customized assessments, and pre-testing. For more information, contact:

NOCTI
500 N. Bronson Ave.
Ferris State University
Big Rapids, MI 49307
(616) 796-4699

*Colleges and universities:*

Many colleges and universities have credit-by-exam programs, through which students earn credit by passing a comprehensive exam for a course offered by the institution. Among the most widely recognized are the programs at Ohio University, the University of North Carolina, Thomas Edison State College, and New York University.

Ohio University offers about 150 examinations for credit. In addition, you may sometimes arrange to take special examinations in non-laboratory courses offered at Ohio University. To take a test for credit, you must enroll in the course. If you plan to transfer the credit earned, you also need written permission from an official at your school. Books and study materials are available, for a cost, through the university. Exams must be taken within 6 months of the enrollment date; most last 3 hours. You may arrange to take the exam off campus if you do not live near the university.

Ohio University is on the quarter-hour system; most courses are worth 4 quarter hours, the equivalent of 3 semester hours. For more information, contact:

Independent Study
Tupper Hall 302
Ohio University
Athens, OH 45701-2979
1(800) 444-2910
(614) 593-2910

The University of North Carolina offers a credit-by-examination option for 140 independent study (correspondence) courses in foreign languages, humanities, social sciences, mathematics, business administration, education, electrical and computer engineering, health administration, and natural sciences. To take an exam, you must request and receive approval from both the course instructor and the independent studies department. Exams must be taken within six months of enrollment, and you may register for no more than two at a time. If you are not near the University's Chapel Hill campus, you may take your exam under supervision at an accredited college, university, community college, or technical institute. For more information, contact:

Independent Studies
CB #1020, The Friday Center
UNC-Chapel Hill
Chapel Hill, NC 27599-1020
1(800) 862-5669 / (919) 962-1134

The Thomas Edison College Examination Program offers more than 50 exams in liberal arts, business, and professional areas. Thomas Edison State College administers tests twice a month in Trenton, New Jersey; however, students may arrange to take their tests with a proctor at any accredited American college or university or U.S. military base. Most of the tests are multiple choice; some also include short answer or essay questions. Time limits range from 90 minutes to 4 hours, depending on the exam. For more information, contact:

Thomas Edison State College
TECEP, Office of Testing and Assessment
101 W. State Street
Trenton, NJ 08608-1176
(609) 633-2844

New York University's Foreign Language Program offers proficiency exams in more than 40 languages, from Albanian to Yiddish. Two exams are available in each language: The 12-point test is equivalent to 4 undergraduate semesters, and the 16-point exam may lead to upper level credit. The tests are given at the university's Foreign Language Department throughout the year.

Proof of foreign language proficiency does not guarantee college credit. Some colleges and universities accept transcripts only for languages commonly taught, such as French and Spanish. Nontraditional programs are more likely than traditional ones to grant credit for proficiency in other languages.

For an informational brochure and registration form for NYU's foreign language proficiency exams, contact:

New York University
Foreign Language Department
48 Cooper Square, Room 107
New York, NY 10003
(212) 998-7030

### *Government institutes:*

The Defense Language Institute and Foreign Service Institute administer foreign language proficiency exams for personnel stationed abroad. Usually, the tests are given at the end of intensive language courses or upon completion of service overseas. But some people -- like Jorge, who knows Spanish -- speak another language fluently and may be allowed to take a proficiency exam in that language before completing their tour of duty. Contact one of the offices listed below to obtain transcripts of those scores. Proof of proficiency does not guarantee college credit, however, as discussed above.

To request score reports from the Defense Language Institute for Defense Language Proficiency Tests, send your name, Social Security number, language for which you were tested, and, most importantly, when and where you took the exam to:

Commandant, Defense Language Institute
Attn: ATFL-ES-T
DLPT Score Report Request
Presidio of Monterey
Monterey, CA 93944-5006

To request transcripts of scores for Foreign Service Institute exams, send your name, Social Security number, language for which you were tested, and dates or year of exams to:

Foreign Service Institute
Arlington Hall
4020 Arlington Boulevard
Rosslyn, VA 22204-1500
Attn: Testing Office (Send your request to the attention of the testing office of the foreign language in which you were tested)

**Credit For Experience**

Experiential learning credit may be given for knowledge gained through job responsibilities, personal hobbies, volunteer opportunities, homemaking, and other experiences. Colleges and universities base credit awards on the knowledge you have attained, not for the experience alone. In addition, the knowledge must be college level; not just any learning will do. Throwing horseshoes as a hobby is not likely to be worth college credit. But if you've done research on how and where the sport originated, visited blacksmiths, organized tournaments, and written a column for a trade journal – well, that's a horseshoe of a different color.

Adults attempting to get credit for their experience should be forewarned: Having your experience evaluated for college credit is time-consuming, tedious work – not an easy shortcut for people who want quick-fix college credits. And not all experience, no matter how valuable, is the equivalent of college courses.

Requesting college credit for your experiential learning can be tricky. You should get assistance from a credit evaluations officer at the school you plan to attend, but you should also have a general idea of what your knowledge is worth. A common method for converting knowledge into credit is to use a college catalog. Find course titles and descriptions that match what you have learned through experience, and request the number of credits offered for those courses.

Once you know what credit to ask for, you must usually present your case in writing to officials at the college you plan to attend. The most common form of presenting experiential learning for credit is the portfolio. A portfolio is a written record of your knowledge along with a request for equivalent college credit. It includes an identification and description of the knowledge for which you are requesting credit, an explanatory essay of how the knowledge was gained and how it fits into your educational plans, documentation that you have acquired such knowledge, and a request for college credit. Required elements of a portfolio vary by schools but generally follow those guidelines.

In identifying knowledge you have gained, be specific about exactly what you have learned. For example, it is not enough for Lynette to say she runs a business. She must identify the knowledge she has gained from running it, such as personnel management, tax law, marketing strategy, and inventory review. She must also include brief descriptions about her knowledge of each to support her claims of having those skills.

The essay gives you a chance to relay something about who you are. It should address your educational goals, include relevant autobiographical details, and be well organized, neat, and convey confidence. In his essay, Jorge might first state his goal of becoming an engineer. Then he would explain why he joined the Army, where he got hands-on training and experience in developing and servicing electronic equipment.

This, he would say, led to his hobby of creating remote-controlled model cars, of which he has built 20. His conclusion would highlight his accomplishments and tie them to his desire to become an electronic engineer.

Documentation is evidence that you've learned what you claim to have learned. You can show proof of knowledge in a variety of ways, including audio or video recordings, letters from current or former employers describing your specific duties and job performance, blueprints, photographs or artwork, and transcripts of certifying exams for professional licenses and certification – such as Alice's certification from the American Culinary Federation. Although documentation can take many forms, written proof alone is not always enough. If it is impossible to document your knowledge in writing, find out if your experiential learning can be assessed through supplemental oral exams by a faculty expert.

## Earning a College Degree

Nontraditional students often have work, family, and financial obligations that prevent them from quitting their jobs to attend school full time. Can they still meet their educational goals? Yes.

More than 150 accredited colleges and universities have nontraditional bachelor's degree programs that require students to spend little or no time on campus; over 300 others have nontraditional campus-based degree programs. Some of those schools, as well as most junior and community colleges, offer associate's degrees nontraditionally. Each school with a nontraditional course of study determines its own rules for awarding credit for prior coursework, exams, or experience, as discussed previously. Most have charges on top of tuition for providing these special services.

Several publications profile nontraditional degree programs; see the Resources section at the end of this article for more information. To determine which school best fits your academic profile and educational goals, first list your criteria. Then, evaluate nontraditional programs based on their accreditation, features, residency requirements, and expenses. Once you have chosen several schools to explore further, write to them for more information. Detailed explanations of school policies should help you decide which ones you want to apply to.

Get beyond the printed word – especially the glowing words each school writes about itself. Check out the schools you are considering with higher education authorities, alumni, employers, family members, and friends. If possible, visit the campus to talk to students and instructors and sit in on a few classes, even if you will be completing most or all of your work off campus. Ask school officials questions about such things as enrollment numbers, graduation rate, faculty qualifications, and confusing details about the application process or academic policies. After you have thoroughly investigated each prospective college or university, you can make an informed decision about which is right for you.

### Accreditation

Accreditation is a process colleges and universities submit to voluntarily for getting their credentials. An accredited school has been investigated and visited by teams of observers and has periodic inspections by a private accrediting agency. The initial review can take two years or more.

Regional agencies accredit entire schools, and professional agencies accredit either specialized schools or departments within schools. Although there are no national accrediting standards, not just any accreditation will do. Countless "accreditation associations" have been invented by schools, many of which have no academic programs and sell phony degrees, to accredit themselves. But 6 regional and about 80 professional accrediting associations in the United States are recognized by the U.S. Department of Education or the Commission on Recognition of Postsecondary Accreditation. When checking accreditation, these are the names to look for. For more information about accreditation and accrediting agencies, contact:

> Institutional Participation Oversight Service Accreditation and State Liaison Division
> U.S. Department of Education
> ROB 3, Room 3915
> 600 Independence Ave., SW
> Washington, DC 20202-5244
> (202) 708-7417

Because accreditation is not mandatory, lack of accreditation does not necessarily mean a school or program is bad. Some schools choose not to apply for accreditation, are in the process of applying, or have educational methods too unconventional for an accrediting association's standards. For the nontraditional student, however, earning a degree from a college or university with recognized accreditation is an especially important consideration. Although nontraditional education is becoming more widely accepted, it is not yet mainstream. Employers skeptical of a degree earned in a nontraditional manner are likely to be even less accepting of one from an unaccredited school.

**Program Features**

Because nontraditional students have diverse educational objectives, nontraditional schools are diverse in what they offer. Some programs are geared toward helping students organize their scattered educational credits to get a degree as quickly as possible. Others cater to those who may have specific credits or experience but need assistance in completing requirements. Whatever your educational profile, you should look for a program that works with you in obtaining your educational goals.

A few nontraditional programs have special admissions policies for adult learners like Alice, who plan to earn their GEDs but want to enroll in college in the meantime. Other features of nontraditional programs include individualized learning agreements, intensive academic counseling, cooperative learning and internship placement, and waiver of some prerequisites or other requirements – as well as college credit for prior coursework, examinations, and experiential learning, all discussed previously.

Lynette, whose primary goal is to finish her degree, wants to earn maximum credits for her business experience. She will look for programs that do not limit the number of credits awarded for equivalency exams and experiential learning. And since well-documented proof of knowledge is essential for earning experiential learning credits, Lynette should make sure the program she chooses provides assistance to students submitting a portfolio.

Jorge, on the other hand, has more credits than he needs in certain areas and is willing to forego some. To become an engineer, he must have a bachelor's degree; but because he is accustomed to hands-on learning, Jorge is interested in getting experience as he gains more technical skills. He will concentrate on finding schools with strong cooperative education, supervised fieldwork, or internship programs.

## Residency Requirements

Programs are sometimes deemed nontraditional because of their residency requirements. Many people think of residency for colleges and universities in terms of tuition, with in-state students paying less than out-of-state ones. Residency also may refer to where a student lives, either on or off campus, while attending school.

But in nontraditional education, residency usually refers to how much time students must spend on campus, regardless of whether they attend classes there. In some nontraditional programs, students need not ever step foot on campus. Others require only a very short residency, such as one day or a few weeks. Many schools have standard residency requirements of several semesters but schedule classes for evenings or weekends to accommodate working adults.

Lynette, who previously took courses by independent study, prefers to earn credits by distance study. She will focus on schools that have no residency requirement. Several colleges and universities have nonresident degree completion programs for adults with some college credit. Under the direction of a faculty advisor, students devise a plan for earning their remaining credits. Methods for earning credits include independent study, distance learning, seminars, supervised fieldwork, and group study at arranged sites. Students may have to earn a certain number of credits through the degree-granting institution. But many programs allow students to take courses at accredited schools of their choice for transfer toward their degree.

Alice wants to attend lectures but has an unpredictable schedule. Her best course of action will be to seek out short residency programs that require students to attend seminars once or twice a semester. She can take courses that are televised and videotape them to watch when her schedule permits, with the seminars helping to ensure that she properly completes her coursework. Many colleges and universities with short residency requirements also permit students to earn some credits elsewhere, by whatever means the student chooses.

Some fields of study require classroom instruction. As Jorge will discover, few colleges and universities allow students to earn a bachelor's degree in engineering entirely through independent study. Nontraditional residency programs are designed to accommodate adults' daytime work schedules. Jorge should look for programs offering evening, weekend, summer, and accelerated courses.

## Tuition and Other Expenses

The final decisions about which schools Alice, Jorge, and Lynette attend may hinge in large part on a single issue: Cost. And rising tuition is only part of the equation. Beginning with application fees and continuing through graduation fees, college expenses add up.

Traditional and nontraditional students have some expenses in common, such as the cost of books and other materials. Tuition might even be the same for some courses, especially for colleges and universities offering standard ones at unusual times. But for nontraditional programs, students may also pay fees for services such as credit or transcript review, evaluation, advisement, and portfolio assessment.

Students are also responsible for postage and handling or setup expenses for independent study courses, as well as for all examination and transcript fees for transferring credits. Usually, the more nontraditional the program, the more detailed the fees. Some schools charge a yearly enrollment fee rather than tuition for degree completion candidates who want their files to remain active.

Although tuition and fees might seem expensive, most educators tell you not to let money come between you and your educational goals. Talk to someone in the financial aid department of the school you plan to attend or check your library for publications about financial aid sources. The U.S. Department of Education publishes a guide to Federal aid programs such as Pell Grants, student loans, and work-study. To order the free 74-page booklet, *The Student Guide: Financial Aid from the U.S. Department of Education,* contact:

Federal Student Aid Information Center
P.O. Box 84
Washington, DC 20044
1 (800) 4FED-AID (433-3243)

**Resources**

Information on how to earn a high school diploma or college degree without following the usual routes is available from several organizations and in numerous publications. Information on nontraditional graduate degree programs, available for master's through doctoral level, though not discussed in this article, can usually be obtained from the same resources that detail bachelor's degree programs.

National Learning Corporation publishes study guides for all of these exams, for both general examinations and tests in specific subject areas. To order study guides, or to browse their catalog featuring more than 5,000 titles, visit NLC online at www.passbooks.com, or contact them by phone at (800) 632-8888.

**Organizations**

Adult learners should always contact their local school system, community college, or university to learn about programs that are readily available. The following national organizations can also supply information:

American Council on Education
One Dupont Circle
Washington, DC 20036-1193
(202) 939-9300

Within the American Council on Education, the Center for Adult Learning and Educational Credentials administers the National External Diploma Program, the GED Program, the Program on Noncollegiate Sponsored Instruction, the Credit by Examination Program, and the Military Evaluations Program.

# College-Level Examination Program (CLEP)

## 1. WHAT IS CLEP?

CLEP stands for the College-Level Examination Program, sponsored by the College Board. It is a national program of credit-by-examination that offers you the opportunity to obtain recognition for college-level achievement. No matter when, where, or how you have learned – by means of formal or informal study – you can take CLEP tests. If the results are acceptable to your college, you can receive credit.

You may not realize it, but you probably know more than your academic record reveals. Each day you, like most people, have an opportunity to learn. In private industry and business, as well as at all levels of government, learning opportunities continually occur. If you read widely or intensively in a particular field, think about what you read, discuss it with your family and friends, you are learning. Or you may be learning on a more formal basis by taking a correspondence course, a television or radio course, a course recorded on tape or cassettes, a course assembled into programmed tests, or a course taught in your community adult school or high school.

No matter how, where, or when you gained your knowledge, you may have the opportunity to receive academic credit for your achievement that can be counted toward an undergraduate degree. The College-Level Examination Program (CLEP) enables colleges to evaluate your achievement and give you credit. A wide range of college-level examinations are offered by CLEP to anyone who wishes to take them. Scores on the tests are reported to you and, if you wish, to a college, employer, or individual.

## 2. WHAT ARE THE PURPOSES OF THE COLLEGE-LEVEL EXAMINATION PROGRAM?

The basic purpose of the College-Level Examination Program is to enable individuals who have acquired their education in nontraditional ways to demonstrate their academic achievement. It is also intended for use by those in higher education, business, industry, government, and other fields who need a reliable method of assessing a person's educational level.

Recognizing that the real issue is not how a person has acquired his education but what education he has, the College Level Examination Program has been designed to serve a variety of purposes. The basic purpose, as listed above, is to enable those who have reached the college level of education in nontraditional ways to assess the level of their achievement and to use the test results in seeking college credit or placement.

In addition, scores on the tests can be used to validate educational experience obtained at a nonaccredited institution or through noncredit college courses.

Some colleges and universities may use the tests to measure the level of educational achievement of their students, and for various institutional research purposes.

Other colleges and universities may wish to use the tests in the admission, placement, and guidance of students who wish to transfer from one institution to another.

Businesses, industries, governmental agencies, and professional groups now accept the results of these tests as a basis for advancement, eligibility for further training, or professional or semi-professional certification.

Many people are interested in the examination simply to assess their own educational progress and attainment.

The college, university, business, industry, or government agency that adopts the tests in the College-Level Examination Program makes its own decision about how it will use and interpret the test scores. The College Board will provide the tests, score them, and report the results either to the individuals who took the tests or the college or agency that administered them. It does NOT, and cannot, award college credit, certify college equivalency, or make recommendations regarding the standards these institutions should establish for the use of the test results.

Therefore, if you are taking the tests to secure credit from an institution, you should FIRST ascertain whether the college or agency involved will accept the scores. Each institution determines which CLEP tests it will accept for credit and the amount of credit it will award. If you want to take tests for college credit, first call, write, or visit the college you wish to attend to inquire about its policy on CLEP scores, as well as its other admission requirements.

The services of the program are also available to people who have been requested to take the tests by an employer, a professional licensing agency, a certifying agency, or by other groups that recognize college equivalency on the basis of satisfactory CLEP scores. You may, of course, take the tests SOLELY for your own information. If you do, your scores will be reported only to you.

While neither CLEP nor the College Board can evaluate previous credentials or award college credit, you will receive, with your scores, basic information to help you interpret your performance on the tests you have taken.

## 3. WHAT ARE THE COLLEGE-LEVEL EXAMINATIONS?

In order to meet different kinds of curricular organization and testing needs at colleges and universities, the College-Level Examination Program offers 35 different subject tests falling under five separate general categories: Composition and Literature, Foreign Languages, History and Social Sciences, Science and Mathematics, and Business.

## 4. WHAT ARE THE SUBJECT EXAMINATIONS?

The 35 CLEP tests offered by the College Board are listed below:

**COMPOSITION AND LITERATURE:**
- American Literature
- Analyzing and Interpreting Literature
- English Composition
- English Composition with Essay
- English Literature
- Freshman College Composition
- Humanities

**FOREIGN LANGUAGES**
- French
- German
- Spanish

**HISTORY AND SOCIAL SCIENCES**
- American Government
- Introduction to Educational Psychology
- History of the United States I: Early Colonization to 1877
- History of the United States II: 1865 to the Present
- Human Growth and Development
- Principles of Macroeconomics
- Principles of Microeconomics
- Introductory Psychology
- Social Sciences and History
- Introductory Sociology
- Western Civilization I: Ancient Near East to 1648
- Western Civilization II: 1648 to the Present

**SCIENCE AND MATHEMATICS**
- College Algebra
- College Algebra-Trigonometry
- Biology
- Calculus
- Chemistry
- College Mathematics
- Natural Sciences
- Trigonometry
- Precalculus

**BUSINESS**
- Financial Accounting
- Introductory Business Law
- Information Systems and Computer Applications
- Principles of Management
- Principles of Marketing

CLEP Examinations cover material taught in courses that most students take as requirements in the first two years of college. A college usually grants the same amount of credit to students earning satisfactory scores on the CLEP examination as it grants to students successfully completing the equivalent course.

Many examinations are designed to correspond to one-semester courses; some, however, correspond to full-year or two-year courses.

Each exam is 90 minutes long and, except for English Composition with Essay, is made up primarily of multiple-choice questions. Some tests have several other types of questions besides multiple choice. To see a more detailed description of a particular CLEP exam, visit www.collegeboard.com/clep.

The English Composition with Essay exam is the only exam that includes a required essay. This essay is scored by college English faculty designated by CLEP and does not require an additional fee. However, other Composition and Literature tests offer optional essays, which some college and universities require and some do not. These essays are graded by faculty at the individual institutions that require them and require an additional $10 fee. Contact the particular institution to ask about essay requirements, and check with your test center for further details.

All 35 CLEP examinations are administered on computer. If you are unfamiliar with taking a test on a computer, consult the CLEP Sampler online at www.collegeboard.com/clep. The Sampler contains the same tutorials as the actual exams and helps familiarize you with navigation and how to answer different types of questions.

Points are not deducted for wrong or skipped answers – you receive one point for every correct answer. Therefore it is best that an answer is supplied for each exam question, whether it is a guess or not. The number of correct answers is then converted to a formula score. This formula, or "scaled," score is determined by a statistical process called *equating*, which adjusts for slight differences in difficulty between test forms and ensures that your score does not depend on the specific test form you took or how well others did on the same form. The scaled scores range from 20 to 80 – this is the number that will appear on your score report.

To ensure that you complete all questions in the time allotted, you would probably be wise to skip the more difficult or perplexing questions and return to them later. Although the multiple-choice items in these tests are carefully designed so as not to be tricky, misleading, or ambiguous, on the other hand, they are not all direct questions of factual information. They attempt, in their way, to elicit a response that indicates your knowledge or lack of knowledge of the material in question or your ability or inability to use or interpret a fact or idea. Thus, you should concentrate on answering the questions as they appear to be without attempting to out-guess the testmakers.

## 5. WHAT ARE THE FEES?

The fee for all CLEP examinations is $55. Optional essays required by some institutions are an additional $10.

## 6. WHEN ARE THE TESTS GIVEN?

CLEP tests are administered year-round. Consult the CLEP website (www.collegeboard.com/clep) and individual test centers for specific information.

## 7. WHERE ARE THE TESTS GIVEN?

More than 1,300 test centers are located on college and university campuses throughout the country, and additional centers are being established to meet increased needs. Any accredited collegiate institution with an explicit and publicly available policy of credit by examination can become a CLEP test center. To obtain a list of these centers, visit the CLEP website at www.collegeboard.com/clep.

## 8. HOW DO I REGISTER FOR THE COLLEGE-LEVEL EXAMINATION PROGRAM?

Contact an individual test center for information regarding registration, scheduling and fees. Registration/admission forms can also be obtained on the CLEP website.

## 9. MAY I REPEAT THE COLLEGE-LEVEL EXAMINATIONS?

You may repeat any examination providing at least six months have passed since you were last administered this test. If you repeat a test within a period of time less than six months, your scores will be cancelled and your fees forfeited. To repeat a test, check the appropriate space on the registration form.

## 10. WHEN MAY I EXPECT MY SCORE REPORTS?

With the exception of the English Composition with Essay exam, you should receive your score report instantly once the test is complete.

## 11. HOW SHOULD I PREPARE FOR THE COLLEGE-LEVEL EXAMINATIONS?

This book has been specifically designed to prepare candidates for these examinations. It will help you to consider, study, and review important content, principles, practices, procedures, problems, and techniques in the form of varied and concrete applications.

12. QUESTIONS AND ANSWERS APPEARING IN THIS PUBLICATION

The College-Level Examinations are offered by the College Board. Since copies of past examinations have not been made available, we have used equivalent materials, including questions and answers, which are highly recommended by us as an appropriate means of preparing for these examinations.

If you need additional information about CLEP Examinations, visit www.collegeboard.com/clep.

## THE COLLEGE-LEVEL EXAMINATION PROGRAM

### How The Program Works

CLEP examinations are administered at many colleges and universities across the country, and most institutions award college credit to those who do well on them. The examinations provide people who have acquired knowledge outside the usual educational settings the opportunity to show that they have learned college-level material without taking certain college courses.

The CLEP examinations cover material that is taught in introductory-level courses at many colleges and universities. Faculties at individual colleges review the tests to ensure that they cover the important material taught in their courses. Colleges differ in the examinations they accept; some colleges accept only two or three of the examinations while others accept nearly all of them.

Although CLEP is sponsored by the College Board and the examinations are scored by Educational Testing Service (ETS), neither of these organizations can award college credit. Only accredited colleges may grant credit toward a degree. When you take a CLEP examination, you may request that a copy of your score report be sent to the college you are attending or plan to attend. After evaluating your scores, the college will decide whether or not to award you credit for a certain course or courses, or to exempt you from them. If the college gives you credit, it will record the number of credits on your permanent record, thereby indicating that you have completed work equivalent to a course in that subject. If the college decides to grant exemption without giving you credit for a course, you will be permitted to omit a course that would normally be required of you and to take a course of your choice instead.

### What the Examinations Are Like

The examinations consist mostly of multiple-choice questions to be answered within a 90-minute time limit. Additional information about each CLEP examination is given in the examination guide and on the CLEP website.

### Where To Take the Examinations

CLEP examinations are administered throughout the year at the test centers of approximately 1,300 colleges and universities. On the CLEP website, you will find a list of institutions that award credit for satisfactory scores on CLEP examinations. Some colleges administer CLEP examinations to their own students only. Other institutions administer the tests to anyone who registers to take them. If your college does not administer the tests, contact the test centers in your area for information about its testing schedule.

Once you have been tested, your score report will be available instantly. CLEP scores are kept on file at ETS for 20 years; and during this period, for a small fee, you may have your transcript sent to another college or to anyone else you specify. (Your scores will never be sent to anyone without your approval.)

## APPROACHING A COLLEGE ABOUT CLEP

The following sections provide a step-by-step approach to learning about the CLEP policy at a particular college or university. The person or office that can best assist students desiring CLEP credit may have a different title at each institution, but the following guidelines will lead you to information about CLEP at any institution.

Adults returning to college often benefit from special assistance when they approach a college. Opportunities for adults to return to formal learning in the classroom are now widespread, and colleges and universities have worked hard to make this a smooth process for older students. Many colleges have established special service offices that are staffed with trained professionals who understand the kinds of problems facing adults returning to college. If you think you might benefit from such assistance, be sure to find out whether these services are available at your college.

### How to Apply for College Credit

STEP 1. Obtain the General Information Catalog and a copy of the CLEP policy from the colleges you are considering. If you have not yet applied for admission, ask for an admissions application form too.

Information about admissions and CLEP policies can be obtained by contacting college admissions offices or finding admissions information on the school websites. Tell the admissions officer that you are a prospective student and that you are interested in applying for admission and CLEP credit. Ask for a copy of the publication in which the college's complete CLEP policy is explained. Also get the name and the telephone number of the person to contact in case you have further questions about CLEP.

At this step, you may wish to obtain information from external degree colleges. Many adults find that such colleges suit their needs exceptionally well.

STEP 2. If you have not already been admitted to the college you are considering, look at its admission requirements for undergraduate students to see if you can qualify.

This is an important step because if you can't get into college, you can't get college credit for CLEP. Nearly all colleges require students to be admitted and to enroll in one or more courses before granting the students CLEP credit.

Virtually all public community colleges and a number of four-year state colleges have open admission policies for in-state students. This usually means that they admit anyone who has graduated from high school or has earned a high school equivalency diploma.

If you think you do not meet the admission requirements, contact the admissions office for an interview with a counselor. Colleges do sometimes make exceptions, particularly for adult applicants. State why you want the interview and ask what documents you should bring with you or send in advance. (These materials may include a high school transcript, transcript of previous college work, completed application for admission, etc.) Make an extra effort to have all the information requested in time for the interview.

During the interview, relax and be yourself. Be prepared to state honestly why you think you are ready and able to do college work. If you have already taken CLEP examinations and scored high enough to earn credit, you have shown that you are able to do college work. Mention this achievement to the admissions counselor because it may increase your chances of being accepted. If you have not taken a CLEP examination, you can still improve your chances of being accepted by describing how your job training or independent study has helped prepare you for college-level work. Tell the counselor what you have learned from your work and personal experiences.

STEP 3. Evaluate the college's CLEP policy.

Typically, a college lists all its academic policies, including CLEP policies, in its general catalog. You will probably find the CLEP policy statement under a heading such as Credit-by-Examination, Advanced Standing, Advanced Placement, or External Degree Program. These sections can usually be found in the front of the catalog.

Many colleges publish their credit-by-examination policies in a separate brochure, which is distributed through the campus testing office, counseling center, admissions office, or registrar's office. If you find a very general policy statement in the college catalog, seek clarification from one of these offices.

Review the material in the section of this guide entitled Questions to Ask About a College's CLEP Policy. Use these guidelines to evaluate the college's CLEP policy. If you have not yet taken a CLEP examination, this evaluation will help you decide which examinations to take and whether or not to take the free-response or essay portion. Because individual colleges have different CLEP policies, a review of several policies may help you decide which college to attend.

STEP 4. If you have not yet applied for admission, do so early.

Most colleges expect you to apply for admission several months before you enroll, and it is essential that you meet the published application deadlines. It takes time to process your application for admission; and if you have yet to take a CLEP examination, it will be some time before the college receives and reviews your score report. You will probably want to take some, if not all, of the CLEP examinations you are interested in before you enroll so you know which courses you need not register for. In fact, some colleges require that all CLEP scores be submitted before a student registers.

Complete all forms and include all documents requested with your application(s) for admission. Normally, an admissions decision cannot be reached until all documents have been submitted and evaluated. Unless told to do so, do not send your CLEP scores until you have been officially admitted.

STEP 5. Arrange to take CLEP examination(s) or to submit your CLEP score(s).

You may want to wait to take your CLEP examinations until you know definitely which college you will be attending. Then you can make sure you are taking tests your college will accept for credit. You will also be able to request that your scores be sent to the college, free of charge, when you take the tests.

If you have already taken CLEP examinations, but did not have a copy of your score report sent to your college, you may request the College Board to send an official transcript at any time for a small fee. Use the Transcript Request Form that was sent to you with your score report. If you do not have the form, you may find it online at www.collegeboard.com/clep.

Your CLEP scores will be evaluated, probably by someone in the admissions office, and sent to the registrar's office to be posted on your permanent record once you are enrolled. Procedures vary from college to college, but the process usually begins in the admissions office.

STEP 6. Ask to receive a written notice of the credit you receive for your CLEP score(s).

A written notice may save you problems later, when you submit your degree plan or file for graduation. In the event that there is a question about whether or not you earned CLEP credit, you will have an official record of what credit was awarded. You may also need this verification of course credit if you go for academic counseling before the credit is posted on your permanent record.

STEP 7. Before you register for courses, seek academic counseling.

A discussion with your academic advisor can prevent you from taking unnecessary courses and can tell you specifically what your CLEP credit will mean to you. This step may be accomplished at the time you enroll. Most colleges have orientation sessions for new students prior to each enrollment period. During orientation, students are usually assigned an academic advisor who then gives them individual help in developing long-range plans and a course schedule for the next semester. In conjunction with this counseling, you may be asked to take some additional tests so that you can be placed at the proper course level.

## External Degree Programs

If you have acquired a considerable amount of college-level knowledge through job experience, reading, or noncredit courses, if you have accumulated college credits at a variety of colleges over a period of years, or if you prefer studying on your own rather than in a classroom setting, you may want to investigate the possibility of enrolling in an external degree program. Many colleges offer external degree programs that allow you to earn a degree by passing examinations (including CLEP), transferring credit from other colleges, and demonstrating in other ways that you have satisfied the educational requirements. No classroom attendance is required, and the programs are open to out-of-state candidates as well as residents. Thomas A. Edison State College in New Jersey and Charter Oaks College in Connecticut are fully accredited independent state colleges; the New York program is part of the state university system and is also fully accredited. If you are interested in exploring an external degree, you can write for more information to:

Charter Oak College
The Exchange, Suite 171
270 Farmington Avenue
Farmington, CT 06032-1909

Regents External Degree Program
Cultural Education Center
Empire State Plaza
Albany, New York 12230

Thomas A. Edison State College
101 West State Street
Trenton, New Jersey 08608

Many other colleges also have external degree or weekend programs. While they often require that a number of courses be taken on campus, the external degree programs tend to be more flexible in transferring credit, granting credit-by-examination, and allowing independent study than other traditional programs. When applying to a college, you may wish to ask whether it has an external degree or weekend program.

## Questions to Ask About a College's CLEP Policy

Before taking CLEP examinations for the purpose of earning college credit, try to find the answers to these questions:

1. Which CLEP examinations are accepted by this college?

A college may accept some CLEP examinations for credit and not others - possibly not the one you are considering. The English faculty may decide to grant college English credit based on the CLEP English Composition examination, but not on the Freshman College Composition examination. Or, the mathematics faculty may decide to grant credit based on the College Mathematics to non-mathematics majors only, requiring majors to take an examination in algebra, trigonometry, or calculus to earn credit. For these reasons, it is important that you know the specific CLEP tests for which you can receive credit.

2. Does the college require the optional free-response (essay) section as well as the objective portion of the CLEP examination you are considering?

Knowing the answer to this question ahead of time will permit you to schedule the optional essay examination when you register to take your CLEP examination.

3. Is credit granted for specific courses? If so, which ones?

You are likely to find that credit will be granted for specific courses and the course titles will be designated in the college's CLEP policy. It is not necessary, however, that credit be granted for a specific course in order for you to benefit from your CLEP credit. For instance, at many liberal arts colleges, all students must take certain types of courses; these courses may be labeled the core curriculum, general education requirements, distribution requirements, or liberal arts requirements. The requirements are often expressed in terms of credit hours. For example, all students may be required to take at least six hours of humanities, six hours of English, three hours of mathematics, six hours of natural science, and six hours of social science, with no particular courses in these disciplines specified. In these instances, CLEP credit may be given as 6 hrs. English credit or 3 hrs. Math credit without specifying for which English or mathematics courses credit has been awarded. In order to avoid possible disappointment, you should know before taking a CLEP examination what type of credit you can receive and whether you will only be exempted from a required course but receive no credit.

4. How much credit is granted for each examination you are considering, and does the college place a limit on the total amount of CLEP credit you can earn toward your degree?

Not all colleges that grant CLEP credit award the same amount for individual tests. Furthermore, some colleges place a limit on the total amount of credit you can earn through CLEP or other examinations. Other colleges may grant you exemption but no credit toward your degree. Knowing several colleges' policies concerning these issues may help you decide which college you will attend. If you think you are capable of passing a number of CLEP examinations, you may want to attend a college that will allow you to earn credit for all or most of them. For example, the state external degree programs grant credit for most CLEP examinations (and other tests as well).

5. What is the required score for earning CLEP credit for each test you are considering?

Most colleges publish the required scores or percentile ranks for earning CLEP credit in their general catalog or in a brochure. The required score may vary from test to test, so find out the required score for each test you are considering.

6. What is the college's policy regarding prior course work in the subject in which you are considering taking a CLEP test?

Some colleges will not grant credit for a CLEP test if the student has already attempted a college-level course closely aligned with that test. For example, if you successfully completed English 101 or a comparable course on another campus, you will probably not be permitted to receive CLEP credit in that subject, too. Some colleges will not permit you to earn CLEP credit for a course that you failed.

7. Does the college make additional stipulations before credit will be granted?

It is common practice for colleges to award CLEP credit only to their enrolled students. There are other stipulations, however, that vary from college to college. For example, does the college require you to formally apply for or accept CLEP credit by completing and signing a form? Or does the college require you to validate your CLEP score by successfully completing a more advanced course in the subject? Answers to these and other questions will help to smooth the process of earning college credit through CLEP.

The above questions and the discussions that follow them indicate some of the ways in which colleges' CLEP policies can vary. Find out as much as possible about the CLEP policies at the colleges you are interested in so you can choose a college with a policy that is compatible with your educational goals. Once you have selected the college you will attend, you can find out which CLEP examinations your college recognizes and the requirements for earning CLEP credit.

## DECIDING WHICH EXAMINATIONS TO TAKE

If You're Taking the Examinations for College Credit or Career Advancement:

Most people who take CLEP examinations do so in order to earn credit for college courses. Others take the examinations in order to qualify for job promotions or for professional certification or licensing. It is vital to most candidates who are taking the tests for any of these reasons that they be well prepared for the tests they are taking so that they can advance as rapidly as possible toward their educational or career goals.

It is usually advisable that those who have limited knowledge in the subjects covered by the tests they are considering enroll in the college courses in which that material is taught. Those who are uncertain about whether or not they know enough about a subject to do well on a particular CLEP test will find the following guidelines helpful.

There is no way to predict if you will pass a particular CLEP examination, but answers to the questions under the seven headings below should give you an indication of whether or not you are likely to succeed.

1. Test Descriptions

Read the description of the test provided. Are you familiar with most of the topics and terminology in the outline?

## 2. Textbooks

Examine the suggested textbooks and other resource materials following the test descriptions in this guide. Have you recently read one or more of these books, or have you read similar college-level books on this subject? If you have not, read through one or more of the textbooks listed, or through the textbook used for this course at your college. Are you familiar with most of the topics and terminology in the book?

## 3. Sample Questions

The sample questions provided are intended to be typical of the content and difficulty of the questions on the test. Although they are not an exact miniature of the test, the proportion of the sample questions you can answer correctly should be a rough estimate of the proportion of questions you will be able to answer correctly on the test.

Answer as many of the sample questions for this test as you can. Check your answers against the correct answers. Did you answer more than half the questions correctly?

Because of variations in course content at different institutions, and because questions on CLEP tests vary from easy to difficult - with most being of moderate difficulty - the average student who passes a course in a subject can usually answer correctly about half the questions on the corresponding CLEP examination. Most colleges set their passing scores near this level, but some set them higher. If your college has set its required score above the level required by most colleges, you may need to answer a larger proportion of questions on the test correctly.

## 4. Previous Study

Have you taken noncredit courses in this subject offered by an adult school or a private school, through correspondence, or in connection with your job? Did you do exceptionally well in this subject in high school, or did you take an honors course in this subject?

## 5. Experience

Have you learned or used the knowledge or skills included in this test in your job or life experience? For example, if you lived in a Spanish-speaking country and spoke the language for a year or more, you might consider taking the Spanish examination. Or, if you have worked at a job in which you used accounting and finance skills, Principles of Accounting would be a likely test for you to take. Or, if you have read a considerable amount of literature and attended many art exhibits, concerts, and plays, you might expect to do well on the Humanities exam.

## 6. Other Examinations

Have you done well on other standardized tests in subjects related to the one you want to take? For example, did you score well above average on a portion of a college entrance examination covering similar skills, or did you obtain an exceptionally high score on a high school equivalency test or a licensing examination in this subject? Although such tests do not cover exactly the same material as the CLEP examinations and may be easier, persons who do well on these tests often do well on CLEP examinations, too.

7. Advice

Has a college counselor, professor, or some other professional person familiar with your ability advised you to take a CLEP examination?

If your answer was yes to questions under several of the above headings, you probably have a good chance of passing the CLEP examination you are considering. It is unlikely that you would have acquired sufficient background from experience alone. Learning gained through reading and study is essential, and you will probably find some additional study helpful before taking a CLEP examination.

## If You're Taking the Examinations to Prepare for College

Many people entering college, particularly adults returning to college after several years away from formal education, are uncertain about their ability to compete with other college students. They wonder whether they have sufficient background for college study, and those who have been away from formal study for some time wonder whether they have forgotten how to study, how to take tests, and how to write papers. Such people may wish to improve their test-taking and study skills prior to enrolling in courses.

One way to assess your ability to perform at the college level and to improve your test-taking and study skills at the same time is to prepare for and take one or more CLEP examinations. You need not be enrolled in a college to take a CLEP examination, and you may have your scores sent only to yourself and later request that a transcript be sent to a college if you then decide to apply for credit. By reviewing the test descriptions and sample questions, you may find one or several subject areas in which you think you have substantial knowledge. Select one examination, or more if you like, and carefully read at least one of the textbooks listed in the bibliography for the test. By doing this, you will get a better idea of how much you know of what is usually taught in a college-level course in that subject. Study as much material as you can, until you think you have a good grasp of the subject matter. Then take the test at a college in your area. It will be several weeks before you receive your results, and you may wish to begin reviewing for another test in the meantime.

To find out if you are eligible for credit for your CLEP score, you must compare your score with the score required by the college you plan to attend. If you are not yet sure which college you will attend, or whether you will enroll in college at all, you should begin to follow the steps outlined. It is best that you do this before taking a CLEP test, but if you are taking the test only for the experience and to familiarize yourself with college-level material and requirements, you might take the test before you approach a college. Even if the college you decide to attend does not accept the test you took, the experience of taking such a test will enable you to meet with greater confidence the requirements of courses you will take.

You will find information about how to interpret your scores in WHAT YOUR SCORES MEAN, which you will receive with your score report, and which can also be found online at the CLEP website. Many colleges follow the recommendations of the American Council on Education (ACE) for setting their required scores, so you can use this information as a guide in determining how well you did. The ACE recommendations are included in the booklet.

If you do not do well enough on the test to earn college credit, don't be discouraged. Usually, it is the best college students who are exempted from courses or receive credit-by-examination. The fact that you cannot get credit for your score means that you should probably enroll in a college course to learn the material. However, if your score was close to the required score, or if you feel you could do better on a second try or after some additional study, you may retake the test after six months. Do not take it sooner or your score will not be reported and your fee will be forfeited.

If you do earn the score required to earn credit, you will have demonstrated that you already have some college-level knowledge. You will also have a better idea whether you should take additional CLEP examinations. And, what is most important, you can enroll in college with confidence, knowing that you do have the ability to succeed.

## PREPARING TO TAKE CLEP EXAMINATIONS

Having made the decision to take one or more CLEP examinations, most people then want to know if it is worthwhile to prepare for them - how much, how long, when, and how should they go about it? The precise answers to these questions vary greatly from individual to individual. However, most candidates find that some type of test preparation is helpful.

Most people who take CLEP examinations do so to show that they have already learned the important material that is taught in a college course. Many of them need only a quick review to assure themselves that they have not forgotten some of what they once studied, and to fill in some of the gaps in their knowledge of the subject. Others feel that they need a thorough review and spend several weeks studying for a test. A few wish to take a CLEP examination as a kind of final examination for independent study of a subject instead of the college course. This last group requires significantly more study than those who only need to review, and they may need some guidance from professors of the subjects they are studying.

The key to how you prepare for CLEP examinations often lies in locating those skills and areas of prior learning in which you are strong and deciding where to focus your energies. Some people may know a great deal about a certain subject area, but may not test well. These individuals would probably be just as concerned about strengthening their test-taking skills as they are about studying for a specific test. Many mental and physical skills are used in preparing for a test. It is important not only to review or study for the examinations, but to make certain that you are alert, relatively free of anxiety, and aware of how to approach standardized tests. Suggestions on developing test-taking skills and preparing psychologically and physically for a test are given. The following section suggests ways of assessing your knowledge of the content of a test and then reviewing and studying the material.

## Using This Study Guide

Begin by carefully reading the test description and outline of knowledge and skills required for the examination, if given. As you read through the topics listed there, ask yourself how much you know about each one. Also note the terms, names, and symbols that are mentioned, and ask yourself whether you are familiar with them. This will give you a quick overview of how much you know about the subject. If you are familiar with nearly all the material, you will probably need a minimum of review; however, if less than half of it is familiar, you will probably require substantial study to do well on the test.

If, after reviewing the test description, you find that you need extensive review, delay answering the sample question until you have done some reading in the subject. If you complete them before reviewing the material, you will probably look for the answers as you study, and then they will not be a good assessment of your ability at a later date.

If you think you are familiar with most of the test material, try to answer the sample questions.

Apply the test-taking strategies given. Keeping within the time limit suggested will give you a rough idea of how quickly you should work in order to complete the actual test.

Check your answers against the answer key. If you answered nearly all the questions correctly, you probably do not need to study the subject extensively. If you got about half the questions correct, you ought o review at least one textbook or other suggested materials on the subject. If you answered less than half the questions correctly, you will probably benefit from more extensive reading in the subject and thorough study of one or more textbooks. The textbooks listed are used at many colleges but they are not the only good texts. You will find helpful almost any standard text available to you., such as the textbook used at your college, or earlier editions of texts listed. For some examinations, topic outlines and textbooks may not be available. Take the sample tests in this book and check your answers at the end of each test. Check wrong answers.

## Suggestions for Studying

The following suggestions have been gathered from people who have prepared for CLEP examinations or other college-level tests.

1. Define your goals and locate study materials

First, determine your study goals. Set aside a block of time to review the material provided in this book, and then decide which test(s) you will take. Using the suggestions, locate suitable resource materials. If a preparation course is offered by an adult school or college in your area, you might find it helpful to enroll.

2. Find a good place to study

To determine what kind of place you need for studying, ask yourself questions such as: Do I need a quiet place? Does the telephone distract me? Do objects I see in this place remind me of things I should do? Is it too warm? Is it well lit? Am I too comfortable here? Do I have space to spread out my materials? You may find the library more conducive to studying than your home. If you decide to study at home, you might prevent interruptions by other household members by putting a sign on the door of your study room to indicate when you will be available.

3. Schedule time to study

To help you determine where studying best fits into your schedule, try this exercise: Make a list of your daily activities (for example, sleeping, working, and eating) and estimate how many hours per day you spend on each activity. Now, rate all the activities on your list in order of their importance and evaluate your use of time. Often people are astonished at how an average day appears from this perspective. They may discover that they were unaware how large portions of time are spent, or they learn their time can be scheduled in alternative ways. For example, they can remove the least important activities from their day and devote that time to studying or another important activity.

4. Establish a study routine and a set of goals

In order to study effectively, you should establish specific goals and a schedule for accomplishing them. Some people find it helpful to write out a weekly schedule and cross out each study period when it is completed. Others maintain their concentration better by writing down the time when they expect to complete a study task. Most people find short periods of intense study more productive than long stretches of time. For example, they may follow a regular schedule of several 20- or 30-minute study periods with short breaks between them. Some people like to allow themselves rewards as they complete each study goal. It is not essential that you accomplish every goal exactly within your schedule; the point is to be committed to your task.

5. Learn how to take an active role in studying.

If you have not done much studying for some time, you may find it difficult to concentrate at first. Try a method of studying, such as the one outlined below, that will help you concentrate on and remember what you read.

    a. First, read the chapter summary and the introduction. Then you will know what to look for in your reading.

    b. Next, convert the section or paragraph headlines into questions. For example, if you are reading a section entitled, The Causes of the American Revolution, ask yourself: *What were the causes of the American Revolution?* Compose the answer as you read the paragraph. Reading and answering questions aloud will help you understand and remember the material.

c. Take notes on key ideas or concepts as you read. Writing will also help you fix concepts more firmly in your mind. Underlining key ideas or writing notes in your book can be helpful and will be useful for review. Underline only important points. If you underline more than a third of each paragraph, you are probably underlining too much.

d. If there are questions or problems at the end of a chapter, answer or solve them on paper as if you were asked to do them for homework. Mathematics textbooks (and some other books) sometimes include answers to some or all of the exercises. If you have such a book, write your answers before looking at the ones given. When problem-solving is involved, work enough problems to master the required methods and concepts. If you have difficulty with problems, review any sample problems or explanations in the chapter.

e. To retain knowledge, most people have to review the material periodically. If you are preparing for a test over an extended period of time, review key concepts and notes each week or so. Do not wait for weeks to review the material or you will need to relearn much of it.

Psychological and Physical Preparation

Most people feel at least some nervousness before taking a test. Adults who are returning to college may not have taken a test in many years or they may have had little experience with standardized tests. Some younger students, as well, are uncomfortable with testing situations. People who received their education in countries outside the United States may find that many tests given in this country are quite different from the ones they are accustomed to taking.

Not only might candidates find the types of tests and the kinds of questions on them unfamiliar, but other aspects of the testing environment may be strange as well. The physical and mental stress that results from meeting this new experience can hinder a candidate's ability to demonstrate his or her true degree of knowledge in the subject area being tested. For this reason, it is important to go to the test center well prepared, both mentally and physically, for taking the test. You may find the following suggestions helpful.

1. Familiarize yourself, as much as possible, with the test and the test situation before the day of the examination. It will be helpful for you to know ahead of time:

a. How much time will be allowed for the test and whether there are timed subsections.

b. What types of questions and directions appear on the examination.

c. How your test score will be computed.

d. How to properly answer the questions on the computer (See the CLEP Sample on the CLEP website)

  e. In which building and room the examination will be administered. If you don't know where the building is, locate it or get directions ahead of time.

  f. The time of the test administration. You might wish to confirm this information a day or two before the examination and find out what time the building and room will be open so that you can plan to arrive early.

  g. Where to park your car or, if you wish to take public transportation, which bus or train to take and the location of the nearest stop.

  h. Whether smoking will be permitted during the test.

  i. Whether there will be a break between examinations (if you will be taking more than one on the same day), and whether there is a place nearby where you can get something to eat or drink.

2. Go to the test situation relaxed and alert. In order to prepare for the test:

  a. Get a good night's sleep. Last minute cramming, particularly late the night before, is usually counterproductive.

  b. Eat normally. It is usually not wise to skip breakfast or lunch on the day of the test or to eat a big meal just before the test.

  c. Avoid tranquilizers and stimulants. If you follow the other directions in this book, you won't need artificial aids. It's better to be a little tense than to be drowsy, but stimulants such as coffee and cola can make you nervous and interfere with your concentration.

  d. Don't drink a lot of liquids before the test. Having to leave the room during the test will disturb your concentration and take valuable time away from the test.

  e. If you are inclined to be nervous or tense, learn some relaxation exercises and use them before and perhaps during the test.

3. Arrive for the test early and prepared. Be sure to:

  a. Arrive early enough so that you can find a parking place, locate the test center, and get settled comfortably before testing begins. Allow some extra time in case you are delayed unexpectedly.

  b. Take the following with you:

- Your completed Registration/Admission Form
- Two forms of identification – one being a government-issued photo ID with signature, such as a driver's license or passport
- Non-mechanical pencil
- A watch so that you can time your progress (digital watches are prohibited)
- Your glasses if you need them for reading or seeing the chalkboard or wall clock

    c. Leave all books, papers, and notes outside the test center. You will not be permitted to use your own scratch paper; it will be provided. Also prohibited are calculators, cell phones, beepers, pagers, photo/copy devices, radios, headphones, food, beverages, and several other items.

    d. Be prepared for any temperature in the testing room. Wear layers of clothing that can be removed if the room is too hot but will keep you warm if it is too cold.

4. When you enter the test room:

    a. Sit in a seat that provides a maximum of comfort and freedom from distraction.

    b. Read directions carefully, and listen to all instructions given by the test administrator. If you don't understand the directions, ask for help before test timing begins. If you must ask a question after the test has begun, raise your hand and a proctor will assist you. The proctor can answer certain kinds of questions but cannot help you with the test.

    c. Know your rights as a test taker. You can expect to be given the full working time allowed for the test(s) and a reasonably quiet and comfortable place in which to work. If a poor test situation is preventing you from doing your best, ask if the situation can be remedied. If bad test conditions cannot be remedied, ask the person in charge to report the problem in the Irregularity Report that will be sent to ETS with the answer sheets. You may also wish to contact CLEP. Describe the exact circumstances as completely as you can. Be sure to include the test date and name(s) of the test(s) you took. ETS will investigate the problem to make sure it does not happen again, and, if the problem is serious enough, may arrange for you to retake the test without charge.

## TAKING THE EXAMINATIONS

A person may know a great deal about the subject being tested, but not do as well as he or she is capable of on the test. Knowing how to approach a test is an important part of the testing process. While a command of test-taking skills cannot substitute for knowledge of the subject matter, it can be a significant factor in successful testing.

Test-taking skills enable a person to use all available information to earn a score that truly reflects his or her ability. There are different strategies for approaching different kinds of test questions. For example, free-response questions require a very different tack than do multiple-choice questions. Other factors, such as how the test will be graded, may also influence your approach to the test and your use of test time. Thus, your preparation for a test should include finding out all you can about the test so that you can use the most effective test-taking strategies.

Before taking a test, you should know approximately how many questions are on the test, how much time you will be allowed, how the test will be scored or graded, what types of questions and directions are on the test, and how you will be required to record your answers.

## Taking Multiple-Choice Tests

1. Listen carefully to the instructions given by the test administrator and read carefully all directions before you begin to answer the questions.

2. Note the time that the test administrator starts timing the test. As you proceed, make sure that you are not working too slowly. You should have answered at least half the questions in a section when half the time for that section has passed. If you have not reached that point in the section, speed up your pace on the remaining questions.

3. Before answering a question, read the entire question, including all the answer choices. Don't think that because the first or second answer choice looks good to you, it isn't necessary to read the remaining options. Instructions usually tell you to select the best answer. Sometimes one answer choice is partially correct, but another option is better; therefore, it is usually a good idea to read all the answers before you choose one.

4. Read and consider every question. Questions that look complicated at first glance may not actually be so difficult once you have read them carefully.

5. Do not puzzle too long over any one question. If you don't know the answer after you've considered it briefly, go on to the next question. Make sure you return to the question later.

6. Make sure you record your response properly.

7. In trying to determine the correct answer, you may find it helpful to cross out those options that you know are incorrect, and to make marks next to those you think might be correct. If you decide to skip the question and come back to it later, you will save yourself the time of reconsidering all the options.

8. Watch for the following key words in test questions:

| | | | |
|---|---|---|---|
| all | generally | never | perhaps |
| always | however | none | rarely |
| but | may | not | seldom |
| except | must | often | sometimes |
| every | necessary | only | usually |

When a question or answer option contains words such as always, every, only, never, and none, there can be no exceptions to the answer you choose. Use of words such as often, rarely, sometimes, and generally indicates that there may be some exceptions to the answer.

9. Do not waste your time looking for clues to right answers based on flaws in question wording or patterns in correct answers. Professionals at the College Board and ETS put

a great deal of effort into developing valid, reliable, fair tests. CLEP test development committees are composed of college faculty who are experts in the subject covered by the test and are appointed by the College Board to write test questions and to scrutinize each question that is included on a CLEP test. Committee members make every effort to ensure that the questions are not ambiguous, that they have only one correct answer, and that they cover college-level topics. These committees do not intentionally include trick questions. If you think a question is flawed, ask the test administrator to report it, or contact CLEP immediately.

Taking Free-Response or Essay Tests

If your college requires the optional free-response or essay portion of a CLEP Composition and Literature exams, you should do some additional preparation for your CLEP test. Taking an essay test is very different from taking a multiple-choice test, so you will need to use some other strategies.

The essay written as part of the English Composition and Essay exam is graded by English professors from a variety of colleges and universities. A process called holistic scoring is used to rate your writing ability.

The optional free-response essays, on the other hand, are graded by the faculty of the college you designate as a score recipient. Guidelines and criteria for grading essays are not specified by the College Board or ETS. You may find it helpful, therefore, to talk with someone at your college to find out what criteria will be used to determine whether you will get credit. If the test requires essay responses, ask how much emphasis will be placed on your writing ability and your ability to organize your thoughts as opposed to your knowledge of subject matter. Find out how much weight will be given to your multiple-choice test score in comparison with your free-response grade in determining whether you will get credit. This will give you an idea where you should expend the greatest effort in preparing for and taking the test.

Here are some strategies you will find useful in taking any essay test:

1. Before you begin to write, read all questions carefully and take a few minutes to jot down some ideas you might include in each answer.

2. If you are given a choice of questions to answer, choose the questions you think you can answer most clearly and knowledgeably.

3. Determine in what order you will answer the questions. Answer those you find the easiest first so that any extra time can be spent on the more difficult questions.

4. When you know which questions you will answer and in what order, determine how much testing time remains and estimate how many minutes you will devote to each question. Unless suggested times are given for the questions or one question appears to require more or less time than the others, allot an equal amount of time to each question.

5. Before answering each question, indicate the number of the question as it is given in the test book. You need not copy the entire question from the question sheet, but it will be helpful to you and to the person grading your test if you indicate briefly the topic you are addressing – particularly if you are not answering the questions in the order in which they appear on the test.

6. Before answering each question, read it again carefully to make sure you are interpreting it correctly. Underline key words, such as those listed below, that often appear in free-response questions. Be sure you know the exact meaning of these words before taking the test.

| | | | |
|---|---|---|---|
| analyze | demonstrate | enumerate | list |
| apply | derive | explain | outline |
| assess | describe | generalize | prove |
| compare | determine | illustrate | rank |
| contrast | discuss | interpret | show |
| define | distinguish | justify | summarize |

If a question asks you to outline, define, or summarize, do not write a detailed explanation; if a question asks you to analyze, explain, illustrate, interpret, or show, you must do more than briefly describe the topic.

---

**For a current listing of CLEP Colleges**

**where you can get credit and be tested, write:**

**CLEP, P.O. Box 6600, Princeton, NJ 08541-6600**

**Or e-mail: clep@ets.org, or call: (609) 771-7865**

# PRINCIPLES OF MACROECONOMICS

**Description of the Examination**

The Principles of Macroeconomics examination covers material that is usually taught in a one-semester undergraduate course in this subject. This aspect of economics deals with principles of economics that apply to an economy as a whole, particularly the general price level, output and income, and interrelations among sectors of the economy. The test places particular emphasis on the determinants of aggregate demand and aggregate supply, and on monetary and fiscal policy tools that can be used to achieve particular policy objectives. Within this context, candidates are expected to understand measurement concepts such as gross domestic product, consumption, investment, unemployment, inflation, inflationary gap, and recessionary gap. Candidates are also expected to demonstrate knowledge of the institutional structure of the Federal Reserve Bank and the monetary policy tools it uses to stabilize economic fluctuations and promote long-term economic growth, as well as the tools of fiscal policy and their impacts on income, employment, price level, deficits, and interest rate. Basic understanding of foreign exchange markets, balance of payments, effects of currency, and appreciation and depreciation on a country's imports and exports are also expected.

The examination contains approximately 80 questions to be answered in 90 minutes. Some of these are pretest questions that will not be scored. Any time candidates spend on tutorials and providing personal information is in addition to the actual testing time.

**Knowledge and Skills Required**

Questions on the Principles of Macroeconomics examination require candidates to demonstrate one or more of the following abilities.

- Understanding of important economic terms and concepts
- Interpretation and manipulation of economic graphs
- Interpretation and evaluation of economic data
- Application of simple economic models
- 

The subject matter of the Principles of Macroeconomics examination is drawn from the following topics. The percentages next to the main topics indicate the approximate percentage of exam questions on that topic.

**8-12%    Basic Economic Concepts**

- Scarcity, choice, and opportunity costs
- Production possibilities curve
- Comparative advantage, specialization, and exchange
- Demand, supply, and market equilibrium
- Macroeconomic issues: business cycle, unemployment, inflation, growth

**12-16%    Measurement of Economic Performance**

- National income accounts
  - Circular flow
  - Gross domestic product
  - Components of gross domestic product
  - Real versus nominal gross domestic product

- Inflation measurement and adjustment
  - Price indices
  - Nominal and real values
  - Costs of inflation

- Unemployment
  - Definition and measurement
  - Types of unemployment
  - Natural rate of unemployment

**10-15%** **National Income and Price Determination**

- Aggregate demand
  - Determinants of aggregate demand
  - Multiplier and crowding-out effects

- Aggregate supply
  - Short-run and long-run analyses
  - Sticky versus flexible wages and prices
  - Determinants of aggregate supply

- Macroeconomic equilibrium
  - Real output and price level
  - Short and long run
  - Actual versus full-employment output
  - Economic fluctuations

**15-20%** **Financial Sector**

- Money, banking, and financial markets
  - Definition of financial assets: money, stocks, bonds
  - Time value of money (present and future value)
  - Measures of money supply
  - Banks and creation of money
  - Money demand
  - Money market
  - Loanable funds market

- Central bank and control of the money supply
  - Tools of central bank policy
  - Quantity theory of money
  - Real versus nominal interest rate

**20-30%** **Inflation, Unemployment, and Stabilization Policies**

- Fiscal and monetary policies
  - Demand-side effects
  - Supply-side effects
  - Policy mix
  - Government deficits and debt

- Inflation and unemployment
  - Types of inflation
  - Demand-pull inflation
  - Cost-push inflation
  - The Phillips curve: short run versus long run
  - Role of expectations

**5-10%** **Economic Growth and Productivity**
- Investment in human capital
- Investment in physical capital
- Research and development, and technological progress
- Growth policy

**10-15%** **Open Economy: International Trade and Finance**
- Balance of payments accounts
  - Balance of trade
  - Current account
  - Capital account

- Foreign exchange market
  - Demand for and supply of foreign exchange
  - Exchange rate determination
  - Currency appreciation and depreciation

- Net exports and capital flows
- Links to financial and goods markets

# ECONOMISTS

NATURE OF THE WORK

Economists study the ways a society uses scarce resources such as land, labor, raw materials, and machinery to produce goods and services. They analyze the costs and benefits of distributing and consuming these goods and services. Their research might focus on topics such as energy costs, electronic components production, farm prices, or imports.

Some economists who are primarily theoreticians may develop theories through the use of mathematical models to explain the causes of business cycles and inflation or the effects of unemployment and tax policy. Most economists, however, are concerned with practical applications of economic policy in a particular area, such as finance, labor, agriculture, transportation, energy, or health. They use their understanding of economic relationships to advise business firms, insurance companies, banks, securities firms, industry associations, labor unions, government agencies, and others.

Depending on the topic under study, economists devise methods and procedures for obtaining data they need. For example, sampling techniques may be used to conduct a survey, and econometric modeling techniques may be used to develop projections. Preparing reports usually is an important part of the economist's job. He or she may be called upon to review and analyze all the relevant data, prepare tables and charts, and write up the results in clear, concise language.

Being able to present economic and statistical concepts in a meaningful way is particularly important for economists whose research is policy directed. Market research analysts who work for business firms may be asked to provide management with information to make decisions on marketing and pricing of company products; to look at the advisability of adding new lines of merchandise, opening new branches, or diversifying the company's operations; to analyze the effect of changes in the tax, laws; or to prepare economic and business forecasts. Business economists working for firms that carry on operations abroad may be asked to prepare forecasts of foreign economic conditions.

Economists who work for government agencies assess economic conditions in the United States and abroad and estimate the economic impact of specific changes in legislation or public policy. For example, they may study how changes in the minimum wage affect teenage unemployment. Most government economists are in the fields of agriculture, business, finance, labor, transportation, utilities, urban economics, or international trade. For example, economists in the U.S. Department of Commerce study domestic production, distribution, and consumption of commodities or services; those in the Federal Trade Commission prepare industry analyses to assist in enforcing Federal statutes designed to eliminate unfair, deceptive, or monopolistic practices in interstate commerce; and those in the Bureau of Labor Statistics analyze data on prices, wages, employment, and productivity.

WORKING CONDITIONS

Economists working for government agencies and private firms have structured work schedules. They may work alone writing reports, preparing statistical charts, and using computers and calculators. Or they may be an integral part of a research team. Most work under pressure of deadlines and tight schedules, and sometimes must work overtime. Their routine may be interrupted by special requests for data, letters, meetings, or conferences. Travel may be necessary to collect data or attend conferences.

Economics faculty has flexible work schedules, dividing their time among teaching, research, consulting, and administrative responsibilities.

## EMPLOYMENT

Economists hold about 15,000 jobs. Private industry -- particularly economic and market research firms, management consulting firms, advertising firms, banks, and securities, investment, and insurance companies -- employed over two-thirds of all salaried economists. The remainders were employed by a wide range of government agencies, primarily in the Federal Government. The Department of Labor, Agriculture, and State are the largest Federal employers. About one out of every five economists runs his or her own consulting business. A number of economists combine a full-time job in government or business with part-time or - consulting work in another setting.

Employment of economists is concentrated in large cities. The largest numbers are in New York City and Washington, D.C. Some work abroad for companies with major international operations; for the Department of State and other U.S. Government agencies; and for international organizations.

Besides the jobs described above, an estimated 30,000 persons held economics and marketing faculty positions in colleges and universities.

## TRAINING, OTHER QUALIFICATIONS, AND ADVANCEMENT

A bachelor's degree with a major in economics or marketing is sufficient for many beginning research, administrative, management trainee, and sales jobs. The undergraduate curriculum includes courses such as microeconomics, macroeconomics, business cycles, economic and business history, and economic development of selected areas, money and banking, international economics, public finance, industrial organization, labor economics, comparative economic systems, economics of national planning, urban economic problems, marketing, and consumer behavior analysis. Courses in related disciplines, such as political science, psychology, organizational behavior, sociology, finance, business law, and international relations, are suggested. Because of the importance of quantitative skills to economists, courses in mathematics, business and economic statistics, sampling theory and survey design, and computer science are highly recommended.

Graduate training increasingly is required for most economist jobs and for advancement to more responsible positions. Areas of specialization at the graduate level include advanced economic theory, mathematical economics, econometrics, history of economic thought, and comparative economic systems and planning. Other areas include economic history, economic development, environmental and natural resource economics, industrial organization, marketing, institutional economics, international economics, labor economics, monetary economics, public finance, regional and urban economics, and social policy. Students should select graduate schools strong in specialties in which they are interested. Some schools help graduate students find internships or part-time employment in government agencies, economic consulting firms, financial institutions, or market research firms. Work experience and contacts can be useful in testing career preference and learning about the job market for economists.

In the Federal Government, candidates for entrance positions generally need a college degree with a minimum of 21 semester hours of economics and 3 hours of statistics, accounting, or calculus. However, because competition is keen, additional education or experience may be required.

For a job as a college instructor in many junior colleges and small 4-year schools, a master's degree generally is the minimum requirement. In some colleges and universities, however, a Ph.D. and extensive publication are required for a professorship and for tenure, which are increasingly difficult to obtain.

In government, industry, research organizations, and consulting firms, economists who have a graduate degree usually can qualify for more responsible research and administrative positions. A Ph.D. is necessary for top positions in many organizations. Many corporation and government executives have a strong background in economics or marketing.

Over 1,200 colleges and universities offer bachelor's degree programs in economics and marketing; over 600, masters and about 130, doctoral programs.

Persons considering careers as economists should be able to work accurately with detail since much time is spent on data analysis. Patience and persistence are necessary because economists may spend long hours on independent study and problem solving. At the same time, they must be able to work well with others. Economists must be objective and systematic in their work and be able to express themselves effectively both orally and in writing. Creativity and intellectual curiosity are essential for success in this field, just as they are in other areas of scientific endeavor.

JOB OUTLOOK

Employment of economists is expected to grow at a slower rate than the average for all occupations in the next decade. Most job openings, however, will result from the need to replace experienced economists who transfer to other occupations, or retire or leave the labor force for other reasons.

Opportunities should be best in manufacturing, financial services, advertising agencies, research organizations, and consulting firms, reflecting the complexity of the domestic and international economies and increased reliance on quantitative methods of analyzing business trends, forecasting sales, and planning of purchasing and production. The continued need for economic analyses by lawyers, accountants, engineers, health service administrators, urban and regional planners, environmental scientists, and others will also increase the number of jobs for economists. Little or no change is expected in the employment of economists in the Federal Government – in line with the rate of growth projected for the Federal work force as a whole. Employment of economists in State and local government combined is expected to grow more slowly than the average.

A strong background in economic theory, statistics, and econometrics provides the tools for acquiring any specialty within the field. Those skilled in quantitative techniques and their application to economic modeling and forecasting and market research, including the use of computers, should have the best job opportunities.

Persons who graduate with a bachelor's degree in economics should face very keen competition for the limited number of economist positions for which they qualify. However, many will find employment in government, industry, and business as management or sales trainees, or as research or administrative assistants. Those with strong backgrounds in mathematics, statistics, survey design, and computer science may be hired by private firms for market research work. Those who meet State certification requirements may become high school economics teachers. (For additional information, see the statement on secondary school teachers elsewhere in the Handbook.)

Candidates who hold master's degrees in economics face very strong competition, particularly for teaching positions in colleges and universities. However, some may gain positions in junior and community colleges. Those with a strong background in marketing and finance may have the best prospects in business, banking, advertising, and management consulting firms.

Ph.D.'s are likely to face competition for academic positions, although top graduates from leading universities should have little difficulty in acquiring teaching jobs. Some will have to accept jobs at smaller or lower paying institutions. Ph.D.'s should have favorable opportunities to work as economists in government, industry, educational and research organizations, and consulting firms.

RELATED OCCUPATIONS

Economists are concerned with understanding and interpreting financial matters, among other subjects. Others with jobs in this area include financial managers, financial analysts, accountants and auditors, underwriters, actuaries, securities and financial services sales workers, credit analysts" loan officers, and budget officers.

SOURCES OF ADDITIONAL INFORMATION

National Association for Business Economics,
1223 20th St. NW, Suite 505, Washington, DC 20036 (Internet: http://www.nabe.com)

# HOW TO TAKE A TEST

You have studied long, hard and conscientiously.

With your official admission card in hand, and your heart pounding, you have been admitted to the examination room.

You note that there are several hundred other applicants in the examination room waiting to take the same test.

They all appear to be equally well prepared.

You know that nothing but your best effort will suffice. The "moment of truth" is at hand: you now have to demonstrate objectively, in writing, your knowledge of content and your understanding of subject matter.

You are fighting the most important battle of your life—to pass and/or score high on an examination which will determine your career and provide the economic basis for your livelihood.

What extra, special things should you know and should you do in taking the examination?

I. YOU MUST PASS AN EXAMINATION

A. WHAT EVERY CANDIDATE SHOULD KNOW
Examination applicants often ask us for help in preparing for the written test. What can I study in advance? What kinds of questions will be asked? How will the test be given? How will the papers be graded?

B. HOW ARE EXAMS DEVELOPED?
Examinations are carefully written by trained technicians who are specialists in the field known as "psychological measurement," in consultation with recognized authorities in the field of work that the test will cover. These experts recommend the subject matter areas or skills to be tested; only those knowledges or skills important to your success on the job are included. The most reliable books and source materials available are used as references. Together, the experts and technicians judge the difficulty level of the questions.
Test technicians know how to phrase questions so that the problem is clearly stated. Their ethics do not permit "trick" or "catch" questions. Questions may have been tried out on sample groups, or subjected to statistical analysis, to determine their usefulness.
Written tests are often used in combination with performance tests, ratings of training and experience, and oral interviews. All of these measures combine to form the best-known means of finding the right person for the right job.

## II. HOW TO PASS THE WRITTEN TEST

### A. BASIC STEPS

1) Study the announcement

How, then, can you know what subjects to study? Our best answer is: "Learn as much as possible about the class of positions for which you've applied." The exam will test the knowledge, skills and abilities needed to do the work.

Your most valuable source of information about the position you want is the official exam announcement. This announcement lists the training and experience qualifications. Check these standards and apply only if you come reasonably close to meeting them. Many jurisdictions preview the written test in the exam announcement by including a section called "Knowledge and Abilities Required," "Scope of the Examination," or some similar heading. Here you will find out specifically what fields will be tested.

2) Choose appropriate study materials

If the position for which you are applying is technical or advanced, you will read more advanced, specialized material. If you are already familiar with the basic principles of your field, elementary textbooks would waste your time. Concentrate on advanced textbooks and technical periodicals. Think through the concepts and review difficult problems in your field.

These are all general sources. You can get more ideas on your own initiative, following these leads. For example, training manuals and publications of the government agency which employs workers in your field can be useful, particularly for technical and professional positions. A letter or visit to the government department involved may result in more specific study suggestions, and certainly will provide you with a more definite idea of the exact nature of the position you are seeking.

3) Study this book!

## III. KINDS OF TESTS

Tests are used for purposes other than measuring knowledge and ability to perform specified duties. For some positions, it is equally important to test ability to make adjustments to new situations or to profit from training. In others, basic mental abilities not dependent on information are essential. Questions which test these things may not appear as pertinent to the duties of the position as those which test for knowledge and information. Yet they are often highly important parts of a fair examination. For very general questions, it is almost impossible to help you direct your study efforts. What we can do is to point out some of the more common of these general abilities needed in public service positions and describe some typical questions.

1) General information

Broad, general information has been found useful for predicting job success in some kinds of work. This is tested in a variety of ways, from vocabulary lists to questions about current events. Basic background in some field of work, such as sociology or economics, may be sampled in a group of questions. Often these are principles which have become familiar to most persons through exposure rather than through formal training. It is difficult to advise you how to study for these questions; being alert to the world around you is our best suggestion.

2) Verbal ability

An example of an ability needed in many positions is verbal or language ability. Verbal ability is, in brief, the ability to use and understand words. Vocabulary and grammar tests are typical measures of this ability. Reading comprehension or paragraph interpretation questions are common in many kinds of civil service tests. You are given a paragraph of written material and asked to find its central meaning.

## IV. KINDS OF QUESTIONS

1. Multiple-choice Questions

Most popular of the short-answer questions is the "multiple choice" or "best answer" question. It can be used, for example, to test for factual knowledge, ability to solve problems or judgment in meeting situations found at work.

A multiple-choice question is normally one of three types:
- It can begin with an incomplete statement followed by several possible endings. You are to find the one ending which best completes the statement, although some of the others may not be entirely wrong.
- It can also be a complete statement in the form of a question which is answered by choosing one of the statements listed.
- It can be in the form of a problem – again you select the best answer.

Here is an example of a multiple-choice question with a discussion which should give you some clues as to the method for choosing the right answer:

When an employee has a complaint about his assignment, the action which will best help him overcome his difficulty is to
    A. discuss his difficulty with his coworkers
    B. take the problem to the head of the organization
    C. take the problem to the person who gave him the assignment
    D. say nothing to anyone about his complaint

In answering this question, you should study each of the choices to find which is best. Consider choice "A" – Certainly an employee may discuss his complaint with fellow employees, but no change or improvement can result, and the complaint remains unresolved. Choice "B" is a poor choice since the head of the organization probably does not know what assignment you have been given, and taking your problem to him is known as "going over the head" of the supervisor. The supervisor, or person who made the assignment, is the person who can clarify it or correct any injustice. Choice "C" is, therefore, correct. To say nothing, as in choice "D," is unwise. Supervisors have and interest in knowing the problems employees are facing, and the employee is seeking a solution to his problem.

2. True/False

3. Matching Questions

Matching an answer from a column of choices within another column.

## V. RECORDING YOUR ANSWERS

Computer terminals are used more and more today for many different kinds of exams.

For an examination with very few applicants, you may be told to record your answers in the test booklet itself. Separate answer sheets are much more common. If this separate answer sheet is to be scored by machine – and this is often the case – it is highly important that you mark your answers correctly in order to get credit.

## VI. BEFORE THE TEST

### YOUR PHYSICAL CONDITION IS IMPORTANT

If you are not well, you can't do your best work on tests. If you are half asleep, you can't do your best either. Here are some tips:

1) Get about the same amount of sleep you usually get. Don't stay up all night before the test, either partying or worrying—DON'T DO IT!
2) If you wear glasses, be sure to wear them when you go to take the test. This goes for hearing aids, too.
3) If you have any physical problems that may keep you from doing your best, be sure to tell the person giving the test. If you are sick or in poor health, you relay cannot do your best on any test. You can always come back and take the test some other time.

Common sense will help you find procedures to follow to get ready for an examination. Too many of us, however, overlook these sensible measures. Indeed, nervousness and fatigue have been found to be the most serious reasons why applicants fail to do their best on civil service tests. Here is a list of reminders:

- Begin your preparation early – Don't wait until the last minute to go scurrying around for books and materials or to find out what the position is all about.
- Prepare continuously – An hour a night for a week is better than an all-night cram session. This has been definitely established. What is more, a night a week for a month will return better dividends than crowding your study into a shorter period of time.
- Locate the place of the exam – You have been sent a notice telling you when and where to report for the examination. If the location is in a different town or otherwise unfamiliar to you, it would be well to inquire the best route and learn something about the building.
- Relax the night before the test – Allow your mind to rest. Do not study at all that night. Plan some mild recreation or diversion; then go to bed early and get a good night's sleep.
- Get up early enough to make a leisurely trip to the place for the test – This way unforeseen events, traffic snarls, unfamiliar buildings, etc. will not upset you.
- Dress comfortably – A written test is not a fashion show. You will be known by number and not by name, so wear something comfortable.
- Leave excess paraphernalia at home – Shopping bags and odd bundles will get in your way. You need bring only the items mentioned in the official notice you received; usually everything you need is provided. Do not bring reference books to the exam. They will only confuse those last minutes and be taken away from you when in the test room.

- Arrive somewhat ahead of time – If because of transportation schedules you must get there very early, bring a newspaper or magazine to take your mind off yourself while waiting.
- Locate the examination room – When you have found the proper room, you will be directed to the seat or part of the room where you will sit. Sometimes you are given a sheet of instructions to read while you are waiting. Do not fill out any forms until you are told to do so; just read them and be prepared.
- Relax and prepare to listen to the instructions
- If you have any physical problem that may keep you from doing your best, be sure to tell the test administrator. If you are sick or in poor health, you really cannot do your best on the exam. You can come back and take the test some other time.

## VII. AT THE TEST

The day of the test is here and you have the test booklet in your hand. The temptation to get going is very strong. Caution! There is more to success than knowing the right answers. You must know how to identify your papers and understand variations in the type of short-answer question used in this particular examination. Follow these suggestions for maximum results from your efforts:

1) Cooperate with the monitor

The test administrator has a duty to create a situation in which you can be as much at ease as possible. He will give instructions, tell you when to begin, check to see that you are marking your answer sheet correctly, and so on. He is not there to guard you, although he will see that your competitors do not take unfair advantage. He wants to help you do your best.

2) Listen to all instructions

Don't jump the gun! Wait until you understand all directions. In most civil service tests you get more time than you need to answer the questions. So don't be in a hurry. Read each word of instructions until you clearly understand the meaning. Study the examples, listen to all announcements and follow directions. Ask questions if you do not understand what to do.

3) Identify your papers

Civil service exams are usually identified by number only. You will be assigned a number; you must not put your name on your test papers. Be sure to copy your number correctly. Since more than one exam may be given, copy your exact examination title.

4) Plan your time

Unless you are told that a test is a "speed" or "rate of work" test, speed itself is usually not important. Time enough to answer all the questions will be provided, but this does not mean that you have all day. An overall time limit has been set. Divide the total time (in minutes) by the number of questions to determine the approximate time you have for each question.

5) Do not linger over difficult questions

If you come across a difficult question, mark it with a paper clip (useful to have along) and come back to it when you have been through the booklet. One caution if you do this – be sure to skip a number on your answer sheet as well. Check often to be sure that you have not lost your place and that you are marking in the row numbered the same as the question you are answering.

6) Read the questions

Be sure you know what the question asks! Many capable people are unsuccessful because they failed to read the questions correctly.

7) Answer all questions

Unless you have been instructed that a penalty will be deducted for incorrect answers, it is better to guess than to omit a question.

8) Speed tests

It is often better NOT to guess on speed tests. It has been found that on timed tests people are tempted to spend the last few seconds before time is called in marking answers at random – without even reading them – in the hope of picking up a few extra points. To discourage this practice, the instructions may warn you that your score will be "corrected" for guessing. That is, a penalty will be applied. The incorrect answers will be deducted from the correct ones, or some other penalty formula will be used.

9) Review your answers

If you finish before time is called, go back to the questions you guessed or omitted to give them further thought. Review other answers if you have time.

10) Return your test materials

If you are ready to leave before others have finished or time is called, take ALL your materials to the monitor and leave quietly. Never take any test material with you. The monitor can discover whose papers are not complete, and taking a test booklet may be grounds for disqualification.

VIII. EXAMINATION TECHNIQUES

1) Read the general instructions carefully. These are usually printed on the first page of the exam booklet. As a rule, these instructions refer to the timing of the examination; the fact that you should not start work until the signal and must stop work at a signal, etc. If there are any special instructions, such as a choice of questions to be answered, make sure that you note this instruction carefully.

2) When you are ready to start work on the examination, that is as soon as the signal has been given, read the instructions to each question booklet, underline any key words or phrases, such as least, best, outline, describe and the like. In this way you will tend to answer as requested rather than discover on reviewing your paper that you listed without describing, that you selected the worst choice rather than the best choice, etc.

3) If the examination is of the objective or multiple-choice type – that is, each question will also give a series of possible answers: A, B, C or D, and you are called upon to select the best answer and write the letter next to that answer on your answer paper – it is advisable to start answering each question in turn. There may be anywhere from 50 to 100 such questions in the three or four hours allotted and you can see how much time would be taken if you read through all the questions before beginning to answer any. Furthermore, if you

come across a question or group of questions which you know would be difficult to answer, it would undoubtedly affect your handling of all the other questions.

4) If the examination is of the essay type and contains but a few questions, it is a moot point as to whether you should read all the questions before starting to answer any one. Of course, if you are given a choice – say five out of seven and the like – then it is essential to read all the questions so you can eliminate the two that are most difficult. If, however, you are asked to answer all the questions, there may be danger in trying to answer the easiest one first because you may find that you will spend too much time on it. The best technique is to answer the first question, then proceed to the second, etc.

5) Time your answers. Before the exam begins, write down the time it started, then add the time allowed for the examination and write down the time it must be completed, then divide the time available somewhat as follows:
   - If 3-1/2 hours are allowed, that would be 210 minutes. If you have 80 objective-type questions, that would be an average of 2-1/2 minutes per question. Allow yourself no more than 2 minutes per question, or a total of 160 minutes, which will permit about 50 minutes to review.
   - If for the time allotment of 210 minutes there are 7 essay questions to answer, that would average about 30 minutes a question. Give yourself only 25 minutes per question so that you have about 35 minutes to review.

6) The most important instruction is to read each question and make sure you know what is wanted. The second most important instruction is to time yourself properly so that you answer every question. The third most important instruction is to answer every question. Guess if you have to but include something for each question. Remember that you will receive no credit for a blank and will probably receive some credit if you write something in answer to an essay question. If you guess a letter – say "B" for a multiple-choice question – you may have guessed right. If you leave a blank as an answer to a multiple-choice question, the examiners may respect your feelings but it will not add a point to your score. Some exams may penalize you for wrong answers, so in such cases only, you may not want to guess unless you have some basis for your answer.

7) Suggestions
   a. Objective-type questions
      1. Examine the question booklet for proper sequence of pages and questions
      2. Read all instructions carefully
      3. Skip any question which seems too difficult; return to it after all other questions have been answered
      4. Apportion your time properly; do not spend too much time on any single question or group of questions
      5. Note and underline key words – all, most, fewest, least, best, worst, same, opposite, etc.
      6. Pay particular attention to negatives
      7. Note unusual option, e.g., unduly long, short, complex, different or similar in content to the body of the question
      8. Observe the use of "hedging" words – probably, may, most likely, etc.

9. Make sure that your answer is put next to the same number as the question
10. Do not second-guess unless you have good reason to believe the second answer is definitely more correct
11. Cross out original answer if you decide another answer is more accurate; do not erase until you are ready to hand your paper in
12. Answer all questions; guess unless instructed otherwise
13. Leave time for review

b. Essay questions
1. Read each question carefully
2. Determine exactly what is wanted. Underline key words or phrases.
3. Decide on outline or paragraph answer
4. Include many different points and elements unless asked to develop any one or two points or elements
5. Show impartiality by giving pros and cons unless directed to select one side only
6. Make and write down any assumptions you find necessary to answer the questions
7. Watch your English, grammar, punctuation and choice of words
8. Time your answers; don't crowd material

8) Answering the essay question

Most essay questions can be answered by framing the specific response around several key words or ideas. Here are a few such key words or ideas:

M's: manpower, materials, methods, money, management
P's: purpose, program, policy, plan, procedure, practice, problems, pitfalls, personnel, public relations

a. Six basic steps in handling problems:
1. Preliminary plan and background development
2. Collect information, data and facts
3. Analyze and interpret information, data and facts
4. Analyze and develop solutions as well as make recommendations
5. Prepare report and sell recommendations
6. Install recommendations and follow up effectiveness

b. Pitfalls to avoid
1. Taking things for granted – A statement of the situation does not necessarily imply that each of the elements is necessarily true; for example, a complaint may be invalid and biased so that all that can be taken for granted is that a complaint has been registered
2. Considering only one side of a situation – Wherever possible, indicate several alternatives and then point out the reasons you selected the best one
3. Failing to indicate follow up – Whenever your answer indicates action on your part, make certain that you will take proper follow-up action to see how successful your recommendations, procedures or actions turn out to be
4. Taking too long in answering any single question – Remember to time your answers properly

# EXAMINATION SECTION

# EXAMINATION SECTION
# TEST 1

DIRECTIONS: Each question or incomplete statement is followed by several suggested answers or completions. Select the one that BEST answers the question or completes the statement. *PRINT THE LETTER OF THE CORRECT ANSWER IN THE SPACE AT THE RIGHT.*

1. Of the following workers, MOST likely to be classified as structurally unemployed would be a

   A. high school teacher who is unemployed during the summer months
   B. recent college graduate who is looking for her first job
   C. teenager who is seeking part-time employment at a fast-food restaurant
   D. worker who is unemployed because his skills are obsolete
   E. woman who reenters the job market after her child begins elementary school

   1.____

2. According to the classical model, an increase in the money supply causes an increase in which of the following?
   I. The price level
   II. Nominal gross national product
   III. Nominal wages
   The CORRECT answer is:

   A. I *only*
   D. II, III
   B. II *only*
   E. I, II, III
   C. III *only*

   2.____

3. If, in response to an increase in investment of $10 billion, equilibrium income rises by a total of $50 billion, then the marginal propensity to save is

   A. 0.1   B. 0.2   C. 0.5   D. 0.8   E. 0.9

   3.____

4. In the circular flow diagram, which of the following is TRUE?

   A. Businesses pay wages, rent, interest, and profits to households in return for use of factors of production.
   B. Businesses purchase goods and services from households in return for money payments.
   C. Households pay wages, rent, interest, and profits to businesses in return for use of factors of production.
   D. The relationship between households and businesses exists only in a traditional society.
   E. The relationship between households and businesses exists only in a command economy.

   4.____

5. Assume that the reserve requirement is 25 percent. If banks have excess reserves of $10,000, the MAXIMUM amount of additional money that can be created by the banking system through the lending process is $_____.

   A. 2,500   B. 10,000   C. 40,000   D. 50,000   E. 250,000

   5.____

6. According to the Keynesian model, an increase in the money supply affects output more if

   6.____

1

A. investment is sensitive to interest rates
B. money demand is sensitive to interest rates
C. the unemployment rate is low
D. consumption is sensitive to the Phillips curve
E. government spending is sensitive to public opinion

7. Which of the following combinations of monetary and fiscal policies is coordinated to increase output?

| | Monetary Policy | Fiscal Policy |
|---|---|---|
| A. | Decrease the reserve requirement | Increase taxes |
| B. | Increase the discount rate | Increase government expenditures |
| C. | Sell securities | Increase taxes |
| D. | Sell securities | Decrease government expenditures |
| E. | Purchase securities | Decrease taxes |

8. Which of the following is a possible cause of stagflation (simultaneous high unemployment and high inflation)?

A. Increase in labor productivity
B. Increase in price for raw materials
C. The rapid growth and development of the computer industry
D. A decline in labor union membership
E. A low growth rate of the money supply

9. If exchange rates are allowed to fluctuate freely and the United States demand for German marks increases, which of the following will MOST likely occur?

A. Americans will have to pay more for goods made in Germany.
B. Germans will find that American goods are getting more expensive.
C. The United States balance-of-payments deficit will increase.
D. The dollar price of marks will fall.
E. The dollar price of German goods will fall.

10. Which of the following would MOST likely be the immediate result if the United States increased tariffs on most foreign goods?

A. The United States standard of living would be higher.
B. More foreign goods would be purchased by Americans.
C. Prices of domestic goods would increase.
D. Large numbers of United States workers would be laid off.
E. The value of the United States dollar would decrease against foreign currencies.

11. Of the following, it is TRUE that a country operating inside its production possibilities frontier

A. has a market economy
B. has a command economy
C. is in the early stages of industrial development
D. is using resources inefficiently
E. has plentiful resources

12. Which of the following is an example of *investment* as the term is used by economists?

    A. A schoolteacher purchases 10,000 shares of stock in an automobile company.
    B. Newlyweds purchase a previously owned home.
    C. One large automobile firm purchases another large automobile firm.
    D. A farmer purchases $10,000 worth of government securities.
    E. An apparel company purchases 15 new sewing machines.

13. If the gross national product increased from $930 billion in 1969 to $975 billion in 1970 solely because of a rise in the price level, which of the following must be TRUE?

    A. Real gross national product increased between 1969 and 1970.
    B. Real gross national product decreased between 1969 and 1970.
    C. Nominal income increased between 1969 and 1970.
    D. Real income increased between 1969 and 1970.
    E. The rise in the price level between 1969 and 1970 was greater than 10 percent.

14. 

    The diagram above shows two aggregate supply curves, $AS_1$ and $AS_2$.
    Which of the following statements MOST accurately characterizes the $AS_1$ curve relative to the $AS_2$ curve?
    $AS_1$.

    A. is Keynesian because it reflects greater wage and price flexibility
    B. is classical because it reflects greater wage and price flexibility
    C. is Keynesian because it reflects less wage and price flexibility
    D. is classical because it reflects less wage and price flexibility
    E. could be either classical or Keynesian because it reflects greater wage flexibility but less price flexibility

15. If the marginal propensity to consume is 0.9, what is the MAXIMUM amount that the equilibrium gross national product could change if government expenditures increase by $1 billion?
    It could _____ by up to $_____ billion.

    A. decrease; 9          B. increase; 0.9          C. increase; 1
    D. increase; 9          E. increase; 10

16.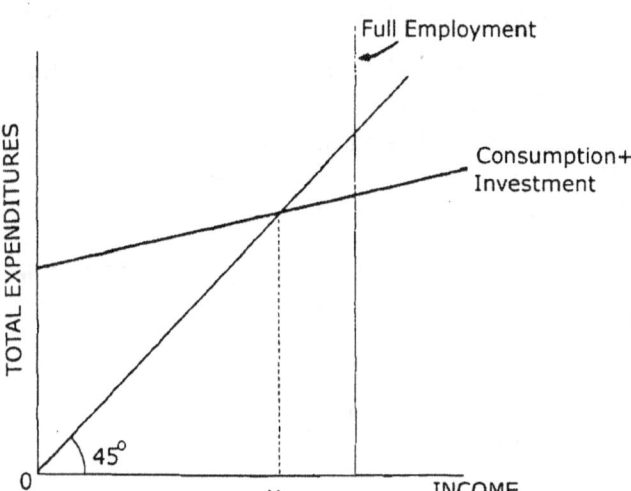

The figure above represents an economy with no government and no foreign sector. Which of the following statements about this economy is TRUE?
At

- A. Y. planned investment is less than saving
- B. Y. planned investment is equal to saving
- C. Y. planned investment is greater than saving
- D. full employment, total spending is equal to total income
- E. full employment, planned investment is equal to saving

17. According to the classical economists, which of the following is MOST sensitive to interest rates?

- A. Consumption
- B. Investment
- C. Government spending
- D. Transfer payments
- E. Intermediate goods

18. Expansionary fiscal policy will be MOST effective when

- A. the aggregate supply curve is horizontal
- B. the economy is at or above full-employment output
- C. transfer payments are decreased, while taxes remain unchanged
- D. wages and prices are very flexible
- E. the Federal Reserve simultaneously increases the reserve requirement

19. Which of the following would increase the value of the multiplier? A(n)

- A. increase in government expenditure
- B. increase in exports
- C. decrease in government unemployment benefits
- D. decrease in the marginal propensity to consume
- E. decrease in the marginal propensity to save

20. According to the monetarists, inflation is MOST often the result of

- A. high federal tax rates
- B. increased production of capital goods

C. decreased production of capital goods
D. an excessive growth of the money supply
E. upward shifts in the consumption function

21. To counteract a recession, the Federal Reserve should    21.____

    A. buy securities on the open market and raise the reserve requirement
    B. buy securities on the open market and lower the reserve requirement
    C. buy securities on the open market and raise the discount rate
    D. sell securities on the open market and raise the discount rate
    E. raise the reserve requirement and lower the discount rate

22. Which of the following would result in the LARGEST increase in aggregate demand?    22.____
    A $30 billion _____ and a $30 billion _____ of government securities.

    A. increase in military expenditure; open-market purchase
    B. increase in military expenditure; open-market sale
    C. tax cut; open-market sale
    D. tax increase; open-market purchase
    E. increase in social security payments; open-market sale

23. Which of the following will be TRUE if inflation can be accurately forecast and both prices    23.____
    and wages are fully flexible?

    A. Long periods of high unemployment will be possible.
    B. The supply of labor will be insensitive to the real wage rate.
    C. The Phillips curve will be vertical.
    D. The equilibrium unemployment rate will be zero.
    E. Real interest rates will be greater than nominal interest rates.

24. Which of the following policies is MOST likely to encourage long-run economic growth in    24.____
    a country?
    A(n)

    A. embargo on high-technology imports
    B. decline in the number of immigrants to the country
    C. increase in government transfer payments
    D. increase in the per capita savings rate
    E. increase in defense spending

25. In one year, real gross national product fell by 3 percent, inflation rose to 10 percent, and    25.____
    unemployment rose to 11 percent.
    Which of the following may have caused these changes?
    A(n)

    A. decrease in the money supply and a decrease in government spending
    B. decrease in inflationary expectations
    C. increase in investment in inventories
    D. increase in the money supply and an increase in government spending
    E. increase in inflationary expectations

## KEY (CORRECT ANSWERS)

| | | | |
|---|---|---|---|
| 1. | D | 11. | D |
| 2. | E | 12. | E |
| 3. | B | 13. | C |
| 4. | A | 14. | C |
| 5. | C | 15. | E |
| 6. | A | 16. | B |
| 7. | E | 17. | B |
| 8. | B | 18. | A |
| 9. | A | 19. | E |
| 10. | C | 20. | D |

21. B
22. A
23. C
24. D
25. E

---

# TEST 2

DIRECTIONS: Each question or incomplete statement is followed by several suggested answers or completions. Select the one that BEST answers the question or completes the statement. *PRINT THE LETTER OF THE CORRECT ANSWER IN THE SPACE AT THE RIGHT.*

1.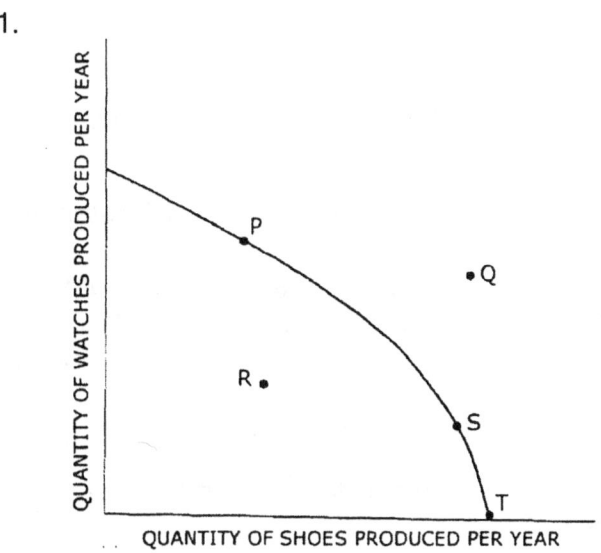

    Which of the following is TRUE of an economy with the production possibilities frontier shown above?

    A. Point Q is attainable but undesirable.
    B. Point R is unattainable but desirable.
    C. A technological improvement in the production of watches would move the economy from point T to point P.
    D. The opportunity cost of moving from point S to point T is the number of watches given up.
    E. There is unemployment at point T because workers in the watch industry are without jobs.

    1.____

2. Increases in real income per capita are made possible by

    A. improved productivity
    B. a high labor/capital ratio
    C. large trade surpluses
    D. stable interest rates
    E. high protective tariffs

    2.____

3. The sum of which of the following expenditures is equal to the value of the gross national product?

    A. Consumer purchases, investment for capital goods, exports, and imports
    B. Consumer purchases, investment for capital goods, net exports, and inventories
    C. Consumer purchases, investment for capital goods, government purchases, and net exports
    D. Consumer purchases, government purchases, exports, and natural income
    E. Investment for capital goods, government purchases, net exports, and inventories

    3.____

7

4. Of the following, MOST likely to lead to a decrease in aggregate demand, that is, shift the aggregate demand curve leftward, would be a(n)

   A. decrease in taxes
   B. decrease in interest rates
   C. increase in household savings
   D. increase in household consumption
   E. increase in business firms' purchases of capital equipment from retained earnings

5. According to the Keynesian model, equilibrium output of an economy may be less than the full-employment level of output because at full employment

   A. sufficient income may not be generated to keep workers above the subsistence level
   B. there might not be enough demand by firms and consumers to buy that output
   C. workers may not be willing to work the hours necessary to produce the output
   D. interest rates might not be high enough to provide the incentive to finance the production
   E. banks may not be willing to lend enough money to support the output

6. The principal reason for requiring commercial banks to maintain reserve balances with the Federal Reserve is that these balances

   A. provide the maximum amount of reserves a bank would ever need
   B. give the Federal Reserve more control over the money-creating operations of banks
   C. ensure that banks do not make excessive profits
   D. assist the Treasury in refinancing government debt
   E. enable the government to borrow cheaply from the Federal Reserve's discount window

7. If the Federal Reserve lowers the reserve requirement, which of the following is MOST likely to happen to interest rates and gross national product?

   |   | Interest Rates | Gross National Product |
   |---|---|---|
   | A. | Increase | Decrease |
   | B. | Increase | Increase |
   | C. | Decrease | Decrease |
   | D. | Decrease | Increase |
   | E. | No change | No change |

8. Which of the following measures might be used to reduce a federal budget deficit?
   I. Raising taxes
   II. Reducing federal spending
   III. Lowering interest rates

   The CORRECT answer is:

   A. I only  B. II only  C. III only
   D. I, III  E. I, II, III

9. If the nominal interest rate is 6 percent and the expected inflation rate is 4 percent, the real interest rate is _____ percent.

   A. 10  B. 6  C. 4  D. 2  E. -2

10. Supply side economists argue that

    A. a cut in high tax rates results in an increased deficit and thus increases aggregate supply
    B. lower tax rates provide positive work incentives and thus shift the aggregate supply curve to the right
    C. the aggregate supply of goods can only be increased if the price level falls
    D. increased government spending should be used to stimulate the economy
    E. the government should regulate the supply of imports

11. If the dollar cost of the British pound decreases, United States imports from and exports to the United Kingdom will change in which of the following ways?

    | | Imports | Exports |
    |---|---|---|
    | A. | Increase | Decrease |
    | B. | Increase | Increase |
    | C. | Increase | No change |
    | D. | Decrease | Decrease |
    | E. | Decrease | Increase |

12. An economy that is fully employing all its productive resources but allocating less to investment than to consumption will be at which of the following positions on the production possibilities curve shown at the right?

    A. A
    B. B
    C. C
    D. D
    E. E

    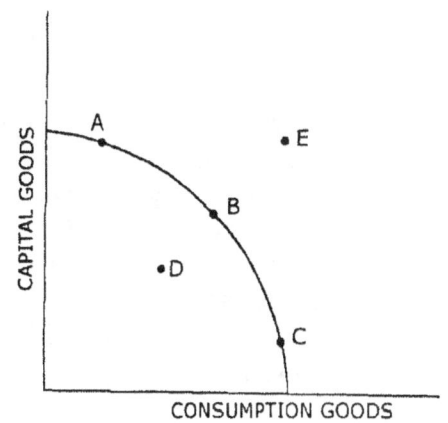

13. The United States government defines an individual as unemployed if the person

    A. does not hold a paying job
    B. has been recently fired
    C. works part-time but needs full-time work
    D. is without a job but is looking for work
    E. wants a job but is not searching because he or she thinks none is available

14. The gross national product is BEST described as a measure of

    A. economic welfare
    B. the full-employment output of an economy
    C. all monetary transactions in an economy
    D. current consumption in an economy
    E. current final output produced by an economy

15. An increase in which of the following would cause the long-run aggregate supply curve to shift to the right?

    A. Corporate income tax rates
    B. Aggregate demand
    C. Potential output
    D. The average wage rate
    E. The price level

16. Total spending in the economy is MOST likely to increase by the largest amount if which of the following occur to government spending and taxes?

    |    | Government Spending | Taxes |
    | --- | --- | --- |
    | A. | Decrease | Increase |
    | B. | Decrease | No change |
    | C. | Increase | Increase |
    | D. | Increase | Decrease |
    | E. | No change | Increase |

17. If businesses are experiencing an unplanned increase in inventories, which of the following is MOST likely to be true?

    A. Aggregate demand is greater than output, and the level of spending will increase.
    B. Aggregate demand is less than output, and the level of spending will decrease.
    C. The economy is growing and will continue to grow until a new equilibrium level of spending is reached.
    D. Planned investment is greater than planned saving, and the level of spending will decrease.
    E. Planned investment is less than planned saving, and the level of spending will increase.

18. The purchase of securities on the open market by the Federal Reserve will

    A. increase the supply of money
    B. increase the interest rate
    C. increase the discount rate
    D. decrease the number of Federal Reserve notes in circulation
    E. decrease the reserve requirement

19. If a banking system's reserves are $100 billion, demand deposits are $500 billion, and the system is fully loaned-up, then the reserve requirement must be _____ percent.

    A. 10    B. 12.5    C. 16.6    D. 20    E. 25

20. According to the Keynesian model, an expansionary fiscal policy would tend to cause which of the following changes in output and interest rates?

    |    | Output | Interest Rates |
    | --- | --- | --- |
    | A. | Increase | Increase |
    | B. | Increase | Decrease |
    | C. | Decrease | Increase |
    | D. | Decrease | Decrease |
    | E. | No change | Decrease |

21. Which of the following policies would MOST likely be recommended in an economy with an annual inflation rate of 3 percent and an unemployment rate of 11 percent? A(n)

    A. increase in transfer payments and an increase in the reserve requirement
    B. increase in defense spending and an increase in the discount rate
    C. increase in income tax rates and a decrease in the reserve requirement
    D. decrease in government spending and the open-market sale of government securities
    E. decrease in the tax rate on corporate profits and a decrease in the discount rate

21.____

22. The cost of reducing unemployment is accepting a higher rate of inflation.
    The statement above would MOST likely be made by a person who believes in the

    A. quantity theory of money
    B. Phillips curve
    C. theory of rational expectations
    D. paradox of value
    E. liquidity trap

22.____

23. Which of the following would occur if the international value of the United States dollar decreased?

    A. United States exports would rise.
    B. More gold would flow into the United States.
    C. United States demand for foreign currencies would increase.
    D. The United States trade deficit would increase.
    E. Americans would pay less for foreign goods.

23.____

24. Which of the following will occur as a result of an improvement in technology?
    The _____ curve will shift _____.

    A. aggregate demand; to the right
    B. aggregate demand; to the left
    C. aggregate supply; to the right
    D. aggregate supply; to the left
    E. production possibilities; inward

24.____

25. Assume that land in an agricultural economy can be used either for producing grain or for grazing cattle to produce beef.
    The opportunity cost of converting an acre from cattle grazing to grain production is the

    A. market value of the extra grain that is produced
    B. total amount of beef produced
    C. number of extra bushels of grain that are produced
    D. amount by which beef production decreases
    E. profits generated by the extra production of grain

25.____

# KEY (CORRECT ANSWERS)

1. D
2. A
3. C
4. C
5. B

6. B
7. D
8. E
9. D
10. B

11. A
12. C
13. D
14. E
15. C

16. D
17. B
18. A
19. D
20. A

21. E
22. B
23. A
24. C
25. D

---

# EXAMINATION SECTION
# TEST 1

DIRECTIONS: Each question or incomplete statement is followed by several suggested answers or completions. Select the one that BEST answers the question or completes the statement. *PRINT THE LETTER OF THE CORRECT ANSWER IN THE SPACE AT THE RIGHT.*

1. What is the present value of $121 to be received one year from now if the rate of interest is 10 percent each year?

    A. $12.10
    B. $100.00
    C. $110.00
    D. $121.00
    E. $133.10

Questions 2-3.

DIRECTIONS: Questions 2 and 3 are to be answered on the basis of the table below, which represents the joint probabilities of a consumer purchasing two products, X and Y.

|  | Purchases Y | Does Not Purchase Y |
|---|---|---|
| Purchases X | .10 | .30 |
| Does Not Purchase X | .40 | .20 |

(e.g., *.30* means that the probability is .3 that a randomly chosen consumer purchases X <u>and</u> does not purchase Y)

2. Given that a consumer purchases Y, what is the probability that the consumer will also purchase X?

    A. .20
    B. .25
    C. .30
    D. .40
    E. .50

3. If X costs $1 per unit and Y costs $2 per unit, what is the expected amount of money spent on the two products by a randomly chosen consumer?

    A. $0.80
    B. $1.00
    C. $1.10
    D. $1.40
    E. $2.00

4. Compared with a large closed economy, a small open economy with a fixed exchange rate will have a _____ domestic multiplier _____ control over the domestic money stock.

    A. smaller; and less
    B. smaller; and more
    C. larger; and less
    D. larger; and more
    E. larger; but the same

5. The imposition of an import tariff will result in which of the following?
    I. A reduction in the volume of world trade
    II. A reduction in the gains from world trade
    III. A distortion in the allocation of resources from that indicated by comparative advantage

    The CORRECT answer is:

    A. I only
    B. II only
    C. I, II
    D. II, III
    E. I, II, III

6.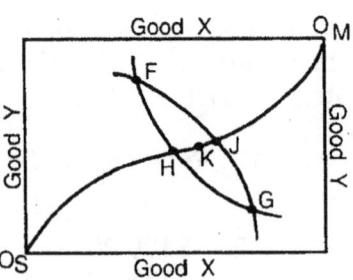

In the above diagram, $O_M O_S$ is the contract curve.

Among the points specifically labeled in the diagram, a Pareto-optimal distribution of goods X and Y between consumers S and M can occur at

A. F only  
B. K only  
C. F or G  
D. H or J  
E. H or J or K

Questions 7-8.

DIRECTIONS: Questions 7 and 8 are to be answered on the basis of the following simple (two-variable) regression model.

$$Y_i = a + bX_i + c_i$$

where

Y = dependent variable  
X = independent variable  
c = disturbance (or error) term  
a, b are parameters  
subscript i refers to the $i^{th}$ observation

7. Which of the following is usually assumed in this model? The

A. expected value of the disturbance term, e, is zero  
B. variance of the disturbance term is unity  
C. variance of the independent variable, X, is unity  
D. dependent variable, Y, is uncorrelated with the disturbance term, e  
E. covariance of the independent variable, X, and the disturbance term, e, is unity

8. If, in addition to the relationship postulated above, the independent variable, X, is a linear function of Y, then which of the following will be TRUE?

A. Autocorrelation will exist among the disturbance terms.  
B. The disturbance terms will be heteroscedastic.  
C. The ordinary least-squares estimators of a and b will be biased.  
D. The estimated standard errors will tend to be quite large because of multi-collinearity.  
E. A dummy variable will be needed to control for this additional relationship.

9. Externalities tend to introduce misallocations of resources into a competitive market system because

   A. individual producers no longer maximize profits
   B. market prices do not accurately reflect true social costs and benefits
   C. balance-of-payments deficits and surpluses generally result
   D. externalities typically result in a more unequal distribution of income
   E. externalities cause unemployment

10. Which of the following policy changes represents an unambiguously contractionary monetary policy?

    |   | Open-Market Operations | Reserve Requirements | Discount Rate |
    | --- | --- | --- | --- |
    | A. | Sale of securities | Increase | Increase |
    | B. | Sale of securities | Increase | Decrease |
    | C. | Purchase of securities | Increase | Increase |
    | D. | Purchase of securities | Decrease | Increase |
    | E. | Purchase of securities | Decrease | Decrease |

11. Which of the following would be MOST likely to induce a monopolist to set an output and a price approachin those that would prevail in a competitive market?

    A. A tax on the monopolist's output
    B. A tax on the monopolist's profits
    C. A subsidy on the monopolist's output
    D. A prescribed minimum selling price for the monopolist's product
    E. Advertising of the monopolist's product

12. It has been estimated that the income elasticity of demand for cars is approximately 1.8. This figure should be interpreted to mean that if income increases by _____ the demand for cars will increase by _____.

    A. 10%; 1.8%      B. 10%; 18%      C. 18%; 10%
    D. $100; $180     E. $180; $100

13. If the level of nominal net national product is rising during a period in which the money supply is constant, which of the following must also be TRUE?

    A. Prices must be rising.
    B. Prices must be constant.
    C. The velocity of money must be rising.
    D. The velocity of money must be constant.
    E. Real net national product must be rising.

Questions 14-15.

DIRECTIONS: Questions 14 and 15 are to be answered on the basis of the following IS-LM digram.

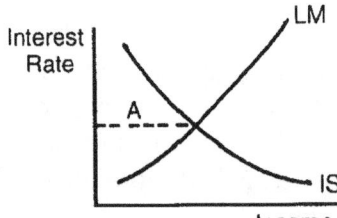

14. At the income-interest rate combination given by point A, there is an excess

    A. supply of goods and an excess supply of money
    B. supply of goods and an excess demand for money
    C. demand for goods, but the money market is in equilibrium
    D. demand for goods and an excess demand for money
    E. demand for goods and an excess supply of money

15. Other things remaining the same, an increase in tax rates causes the equilibrium level of income to

    A. fall and the interest rate to fall
    B. fall and the interest rate to rise
    C. fall, and leaves the equilibrium level of the interest rate unchanged
    D. rise and the interest rate to rise
    E. rise and the interest rate to fall

16. If average total cost increases as output increases, which of the following must be TRUE?

    A. Marginal cost must be constant.
    B. Average fixed cost must be increasing.
    C. Fixed cost must be increasing.
    D. Average variable cost must be greater than average fixed cost.
    E. Marginal cost must be greater than average total cost.

17. If a consumer of two goods possesses indifference curves that have everywhere a constant marginal rate of substitution, the consumer's utility-maximizing purchases will MOST likely include

    A. equal expenditures on both goods
    B. equal amounts of both goods
    C. some of both goods, but in unequal amounts
    D. one good only
    E. unspent income

18. According to the *factor-proportions* argument, urban unemployment may rise during the process of economic development because urban and rural areas use factors in

    A. different proportions and elasticities of substitution are high
    B. different proportions and elasticities of substitution are low
    C. the same proportions and elasticities of substitution are high
    D. the same proportions and elasticities of substitution are low
    E. the same proportions regardless of the elasticities of substitution

19. Which of the following would be a coordinated combination of fiscal and monetary policies instituted to decrease aggregate demand?

|    | Fiscal Policy | Monetary Policy |
|----|---------------|-----------------|
| A. | Decrease in government expenditures | Decrease in reserve requirement |
| B. | Increase in government expenditures | Increase in reserve requirement |
| C. | Decrease in personal income tax rates | Central-bank sale of government securties in the open market |
| D. | Increase in personal income tax rates | Central-bank purchase of government securities in the open market |
| E. | income tax Personal income tax rates | Central-bank sale of government securities in the open market |

Questions 20-21.

DIRECTIONS: Questions 20 and 21 are to be answered on the basis of the following demand and cost functions for a good.

$$P = 20 - 0.5Q$$
$$C = 75 + 5Q$$

where

$P$ = price
$Q$ = quantity
$C$ = total cost

20. The level of output of a profit-maximizing monopolist would be

    A. 5    B. 10    C. 15    D. 20    E. 30

21. If the rest of the economy is perfectly competitive, the level of output that would achieve optimal use of resources would be

    A. 5    B. 10    C. 15    D. 20    E. 30

22. Which of the following did NOT contribute to the eighteenth-century Industrial Revolution in Britain?

    A. Rapid technological change in the textile industry
    B. Enclosure and consolidation of agricultural lands
    C. Introduction of gold as a convenient medium of exchange
    D. Increased trade with other nations
    E. Invention and application of the steam engine

23. Assume that the population is growing at 2 percent per year and that the capital output ratio is 4 to 1.
    Approximately what percent of gross national product must be saved and invested if per capita output is to rise by 1 percent per year?

    A. 6%    B. 8%    C. 9%    D. 12%    E. 16%

Questions 24-25.

DIRECTIONS: Questions 24 and 25 are to be answered on the basis of the following Cobb-Douglas production function.

$$Q = AK^a L^{1-a}$$

where
- $Q$ = output
- $K$ = capital
- $L$ = labor
- $A$ = a constant, where $A>0$
- $a$ = a constant, where $0<a<1$

24. In this production function, the marginal product of labor is equal to

    A. K/L  B. (1-a)  C. A
    D. a(Q/K)  E. (1-a)(Q/L)

25. Which of the following statements concerning this production function is FALSE?

    A. The production function is homogeneous of degree one.
    B. For given prices of K and L, the long-run average cost curve is U-shaped.
    C. For a given K, the marginal physical product of L will decrease when L is
    D. At given prices for K and L, factor proportions are independent of the level of output.
    E. If the firm is a perfect competitor in factor and final product markets, its equilibrium size is indeterminate.

26. Two countries, T and Z, produce only two goods, cloth and meat, using labor as the only input. Each country has 100 workers. The production processes in both countries are subject to constant returns to scale. The table below shows the maximum daily output of each commodity in each country if all of that country's labor is allocated to industry.

    | Country | Cloth(yards) | Meat(pounds) |
    | --- | --- | --- |
    | T | 10 | 30 |
    | Z | 20 | 40 |

    Which of the following statements is(are) correct?
    I. Z has a comparative advantage in meat.
    II. Z has a comparative advantage in cloth.
    III. Z has an absolute advantage in both goods.
    The CORRECT answer is:

    A. I only  B. II only  C. III only
    D. I, II   E. II, III

Questions 27-28.

DIRECTIONS: Questions 27 and 28 are to be answered on the basis of the following macro-model of a closed economy. All data are in billions of dollars.

$$Y = C + I + G$$
$$C = .8(Y-T)$$
$$I = 40 + .1Y$$
where

Y = income  G = government expenditures
C = consumption  T = taxes
I = investment

27. If there are no taxes or government expenditures, what is the equilibrium level of national income?
    _____ billion.
    A. $60  B. $100  C. $400  D. $500  E. $800

28. Now assume the government levies an income tax of 25 percent and simultaneously undertakes expenditures in an amount that balances the budget.
    What is the equilibrium level of national income?
    _____ billion.
    A. $200  B. $400  C. $600  D. $800  E. $1,200

29. An entrepreneur reports, *I'm losing money but I am not shutting down.*
    Given that the entrepreneur's firm is attempting to maximize profits in the short run, this reaction is

    A. rational if the firm is covering its variable costs
    B. rational if the firm is covering its fixed costs
    C. rational if the firm's expectations are rational
    D. irrational since the firm will not have to incur fixed costs when the plant is shut down
    E. irrational since closing the plant is necessary to eliminate losses

30. In a typical set of national income and product accounts in the absence of a government sector, the sum of factor incomes equals the value of total output because

    A. factor shares sum to unity with a Cobb-Douglas production function
    B. net worth is a balance-sheet residual that ensures equality
    C. profits are a residual equal to the value of output minus payments to other factors
    D. investment is equal to savings plus depreciation
    E. expenditures by consumers are equal to wage payments to workers

31. A person sells $100,000 in government bonds to the central bank.
    If the person puts the cash proceeds in a safe-deposit box, then the money supply (MI) will

    A. be unchanged and the supply of bank reserves will also remain the same
    B. be unchanged but the supply of bank reserves will increase by $100,000
    C. increase by $100,000
    D. increase by some multiple of $100,000 that will depend on the legal reserve ratio
    E. decrease by $100,000 because the proceeds have been removed from circulation

## KEY (CORRECT ANSWERS)

| | | | |
|---|---|---|---|
| 1. | C | 16. | E |
| 2. | A | 17. | D |
| 3. | D | 18. | B |
| 4. | A | 19. | E |
| 5. | E | 20. | C |
| 6. | E | 21. | E |
| 7. | A | 22. | C |
| 8. | C | 23. | D |
| 9. | B | 24. | E |
| 10. | A | 25. | B |
| 11. | C | 26. | E |
| 12. | B | 27. | C |
| 13. | C | 28. | D |
| 14. | E | 29. | A |
| 15. | A | 30. | C |
| | | 31. | C |

# EXAMINATION SECTION
# TEST 1

DIRECTIONS: Each question or incomplete statement is followed by several suggested answers or completions. Select the one that BEST answers the question or completes the statement. *PRINT THE LETTER OF THE CORRECT ANSWER IN THE SPACE AT THE RIGHT.*

1. WHICH of the following are examples of leakage from the circular flow of money?   1.____
    - I. Personal savings
    - II. Business savings
    - III. Government expenditures
    - IV. Exports
    - V. Tax collections

    The *CORRECT* answer is:

    A. I, IV  
    D. III, IV, V  
    B. I, II, V  
    E. III, IV  
    C. I, IV, V

2. *WHAT* is the MAIN difference between "token coins" and "full-bodied money"? They   2.____

    A. are metal  
    B. are less valuable  
    C. are marked with a sign of authority  
    D. bear a distinguishing mark  
    E. show no difference

3. The *BULK* of money in the United States is in the form of   3.____

    A. coins and paper money  
    B. time deposits  
    C. demand deposits  
    D. cash value of insurance policies  
    E. savings and loan association shares

4. *HOW* do commercial banks differ from other financial institutions? They can   4.____

    A. handle time deposits  
    B. invest in government securities  
    C. channel the savings of households into private investment  
    D. issue currency  
    E. create money

5. *WHAT* is (are) the component(s) of currency?   5.____
    - I. Federal Reserve notes
    - II. Coins
    - III. Silver dollars
    - IV. Silver certificates
    - V. U.S. notes

    The *CORRECT* answer is:

    A. I *only*  
    C. I, IV, V  
    E. All of the above  
    B. II, III  
    D. I, II, III, V

21

6. The Keynesian "liquidity trap" defines a situation wherein 6.____

   A. suppliers of money compete in the market for loanable funds
   B. disposable money is kept from responding to changes in the GNP
   C. firms and households do not invest excessive money
   D. investors are induced to borrow more money in order to invest more
   E. the interest elasticity of investment and consumption is small

7. WHAT the consuming sector of the economy spends is called 7.____

   A. consumption          B. net investment
   C. expenditures         D. disposable income
   E. net transfers

8. WHICH economy is the BEST example of hyperinflation? 8.____

   A. Germany following World War I
   B. Russia following the 1917 Revolution
   C. Great Britain following World War II
   D. the United States following the Korean War
   E. the United States following the Vietnam War

9. WHAT are the "dependent" variables of macroeconomic theory? 9.____
   I. The rate of change in the general price level
   II. Changes in the production function
   III. Changes in unemployment
   IV. Changes in the aggregate supply function
   V. Changes in population

   The CORRECT answer is:

   A. I, II, IV        B. I, III         C. II, IV, V
   D. I, III, V        E. II, IV

10. WHAT causes structural-demand inflation? When 10.____

    A. the purchasing power of money and government bonds in the hands of the private sector increases
    B. prices in industries with weak demand do not decline
    C. prices rise even though producers cannot meet demand
    D. entrepreneurs increase investment
    E. the government boosts aggregate demand

11. WHAT is the basic principle of the stabilization policy of the "Swedish budget"? That 11.____

    A. government expenditures should be solely determined by public needs
    B. an index of economic activity should be designed
    C. consumption is a stable function
    D. technological innovation is external to the economic system
    E. interest rates should not be manipulated

12. HOW does the stabilization theory of "formula flexibility" attempt to stabilize the economy? By

    A. discretionary tax reductions or increases in government expenditures
    B. having the central bank dominate the level of the monetary base
    C. having tax rates automatically respond to changes in economic activity
    D. manipulating the stock of money
    E. having money accelerate and decelerate according to economic cycles

13. WHAT are the drawbacks to the gold-flow mechanism to correct trade imbalances? It
    I. results in nations exporting unemployment problems to others
    II. relies on inflation and deflation
    III. relies on price levels that may not respond quickly enough to gold movements
    IV. relies on currency valuation changes
    V. relies on speculative movements of capital

    The CORRECT answer is:

    A. I, IV
    B. I, V
    C. I, IV, V
    D. II, III
    E. IV, V

14. WHICH of the following give rise to the purchase of foreign currency?
    I. Capital imports
    II. Foreign aid
    III. Tourism in the United States
    IV. News that the government intends to devalue the currency
    V. U.S. military personnel stationed in foreign countries

    The CORRECT answer is:

    A. I, V
    B. III, IV
    C. I, II, IV
    D. II, III, IV
    E. I, IV, V

15. WHAT is "hot money"?

    A. Capital used for speculation prior to and after a devaluation of currency
    B. Capital used to purchase future foreign currencies
    C. The external price of currency
    D. Currency loaned by the International Monetary Fund
    E. Undesirable currency

16. WHAT IS the ONLY REAL SERVICE rendered by gold in a modern economy? It

    A. *facilitates* foreign trade
    B. *determines* the supply of money
    C. *gives* currency value
    D. *deters* economic cycles
    E. *produces* a value that is constant

17. WHAT is the speciality of mutual savings banks?

    A. Investments in government securities
    B. Checking accounts
    C. Investments in residential construction
    D. Long-term loans
    E. Investments in real estate

18. WHICH of the following motives for holding money is(are) NEGATIVELY related to the interest rate? The _____ motive.

   A. precautionary motive and the speculative
   B. speculative
   C. transactions motive and the speculative
   D. transactions motive and the precautionary
   E. transactions

19. The CHIEF item separating net national product from disposable income is

   A. depreciation
   B. retained earnings
   C. transfer payments
   D. expenditures
   E. net taxes

20. HOW does the government increase the high-powered money in the economy? By

   A. printing money
   B. selling bonds to the central bank
   C. changing government spending and the level of taxes
   D. selling securities to the private sector
   E. generating optimism in the business and financial communities

21. WHAT is the central variation in macroeconomic theory that explains changes in unemployment and inflation? Variation in the

   A. production function
   B. aggregate-supply function
   C. efficiency-change function
   D. growth rate of real output
   E. labor force participation function

22. WHAT is the GREATEST impediment to a smoothly functioning stabilization policy in the United States?

   A. The increase of union strength within the economy
   B. Continued growth of the public debt
   C. Social considerations
   D. Timing the implementation of stabilizing tools
   E. Lack of knowledge of factors affecting investment

23. WHAT is the basic principle of the stabilization policy of "formula flexibility"?

   A. That for each debtor there is a creditor
   B. To promote maximum employment
   C. To determine the velocity of circulation
   D. Delegating limited powers of changing tax rates to the Executive Branch
   E. To design an index of economic activity

24. WHAT is the MAIN advantage of the stabilization policy of "formula flexibility"? It

   A. smoothes the ups and downs of economic activity
   B. provides actual measurement of the macroeconomic variables
   C. provides a formula that separates the rise in price from the rise in quality

D. provides a method of estimating the potential GNP
E. is divorced from political arbitrariness

25. WHICH of the following describes devaluation without depreciation? It is a

   A. situation wherein price changes increase exports
   B. situation wherein the value of one country's currency declines relative to another country's
   C. process of changing price levels until a relative price level occurs
   D. situation that leads to higher levels of domestic production at the expense of foreign goods
   E. process akin to printing high-powered money

26. WHICH of the following factors RAISE the price of foreign currency?
   I. Economic expansion and boom within the United States
   II. A change in the tastes of foreign consumers in favor of American commodities
   III. A change in the tastes of foreign entrepreneurs in favor of investing in the United States
   IV. Technological changes within the United States
   V. Increased investment abroad

   The CORRECT answer is:

   A. I, II, III         B. III, IV, V         C. II, III
   D. II, III, IV        E. I, V

27. WHAT meaning does "hedging" have in international trade? It means

   A. purchasers refuse to commit themselves in advance to a purchase
   B. purchasing future foreign currency at a predetermined rate of exchange
   C. sellers will only accept hard currency for purchases
   D. purchasers fixing the price of an item at the time the order is placed
   E. methods used to guard against increased outflows of capital

28. WHY should a government HESITATE to counter depressionary tendencies by devaluating its currency? It

   A. changes price levels
   B. decreases exports
   C. adversely affects international harmony and goodwill
   D. cures one problem at the expense of the entire economy
   E. causes nations to retaliate by imposing strict controls on movements of commodities and capital

29. The monetarist or traditional approach to stabilization emphasizes the role played by the

   A. Council of Economic Advisors
   B. Congress
   C. Federal Reserve Board
   D. public and commercial banking system
   E. Joint Economic Committee of Congress

30. A growing public debt

    A. is evidence of government mismanagement
    B. is a burden for future generations
    C. impedes a smoothly functioning stabilization policy
    D. does not cause instability or interfere with policies to stabilize the economy
    E. inhibits the economy's long-run tendency to expand

31. *WHICH* of the following are TRUE of the American economy?
    I. Stable total demand is never produced by the American system
    II. Short-run fluctuations of total demand are influenced by changes in business investment expenditures
    III. The mechanism setting boundaries to short-run fluctuations are inherent in the system
    IV. Changes in interest rates are largely explained by changes in the rate of increase of the money supply
    V. The market economy is generally capable of self-feeding change in total demand in either direction without limit

    The *CORRECT* answer is:

    A. I, III, IV    B. I, II, V    C. II, III, IV
    D. II, V         E. I, II, IV

32. Macroeconomic theory is the theory of all of the following *EXCEPT*

    A. prices
    B. money
    C. production and consumption
    D. employment
    E. income

33. During a "repressed inflation," inflationary pressures are repressed by

    A. limited excess reserves of commercial banks
    B. forced saving
    C. the amount of money held for transaction purposes
    D. a low rate of interest
    E. a lack of high-powered money in the economy

34. The "Pigou Effect" is based on the fact that

    A. for each debtor there is a creditor
    B. supply creates its own demand
    C. investment is proportional to changes in output
    D. desired capital is a function of the level of output
    E. government debt is held by financial institutions and firms all over the country

35. *WHAT* is the *ESSENTIAL* role of the central bank? To

    A. *create* money
    B. *regulate* the amount of currency in circulation
    C. *establish* interest rates
    D. *regulate* the supply of money in the economy
    E. *align* prices with money supplies

36. The "stock of money" is the sum of
    I. currency in circulation
    II. demand deposits in commercial banks
    III. U.S. bonds
    IV. time deposits
    V. certificates of deposit
    
    The CORRECT answer is:
    
    A. I, II
    B. I, III
    C. I, IV
    D. I, II, IV
    E. All of the above

37. According to the classical economists, WHAT brings the market for funds into equilibrium? The
    
    A. interest rate
    B. quantity of money supplied by savers
    C. composition of the market for funds
    D. number of investors
    E. difference between the number of investors and the number of savers

38. The proportion of consumption to disposable personal income
    
    A. decreases with the growth of income per capita over time
    B. has changed significantly since the Great Depression
    C. increases even with a decline of income per capita over time
    D. does not diminish over time in spite of the growth of income per capita over time
    E. is dependent upon the GNP

39. WHICH of the following is (are) unconditionally legal tender?
    I. Time deposits
    II. Demand deposits
    III. U.S. bonds
    IV. Coins
    V. Paper money
    
    The CORRECT answer is:
    
    A. I, II, IV, V
    B. III, IV, V
    C. IV only
    D. V only
    E. None of the above

40. WHAT is the speciality of savings and loan associations?
    
    A. Transferring savings to investment in real estate
    B. Time deposits
    C. Long-term loans
    D. Investment in private business
    E. Demand deposits

41. WHAT is the "public debt"? The unpaid amount
    
    A. the public has borrowed
    B. business firms have borrowed
    C. the federal government has borrowed
    D. commercial banks have borrowed
    E. the public and business firms have borrowed

42. WHEN is an economic stabilizer considered to be "built-in" to the system? When          42.____

    A. laws exist to govern phases of the cycle
    B. it begins to operate automatically over the cycle
    C. it promotes maximum employment
    D. it is easily set in motion
    E. it is impervious to economic changes

43. WHAT explains the response of output and price level to any given growth rate of total          43.____
    demand? The theory of

    A. real output
    B. production
    C. economic development
    D. total demand
    E. the aggregate-supply function

44. WHICH of the following are true when American exports fall short of American imports?          44.____
    It leads to
        I.   a reduction in gold reserves of the Federal Reserve System
        II.  a reduction in the foreign currency reserves of the Federal Reserve System
        III. an increase in the purchase of foreign currency
        IV.  a decrease in the purchase of foreign currency
        V.   the imposition of administrative controls on exports
    The CORRECT answer is:

    A. I, II, III          B. I, II, IV          C. II, V
    D. I, IV, V            E. I, II, V

45. WHAT is an objection to a flexible exchange rate? It          45.____

    A. can cause governments to impose administrative restrictions on trade
    B. interferes with the price of currency being determined in the free market
    C. causes the central bank to synchronize the inflow and outflow of foreign currencies
    D. gives rise to inflationary pressures
    E. could lead to a reduced level of world trade

46. Macroeconomic theory and practice is largely influenced by          46.____

    A. international trade
    B. political implications
    C. differences between economists
    D. public opinion
    E. available information

47. WHICH of the following is (are) the preferred method of the Federal Reserve System for          47.____
    changing the economy's supply of money?

    A. Open market operations
    B. Discounting policies
    C. Changing the reserve ratio
    D. Discounting policies and changing the reserve ratio
    E. Open market operations and discounting policies

48. Currency consists PRIMARILY of

    A. coins
    B. silver dollars
    C. silver certificates
    D. U.S. notes
    E. Federal Reserve notes

49. WHAT was the MAIN disadvantage of the gold standard?

    A. The supply of money was limited by legislation
    B. The supply of money was not determined by the needs of the economy
    C. Changing gold supplies caused inflations and recessions
    D. It limited the supply of money
    E. Prices were unable to adjust to fluctuations in gold production

50. The ratio Disposable Personal Income to Gross National Product is determined to a very large extent by

    A. financial institutions
    B. the government
    C. the flexibility of prices
    D. consumers
    E. the net export of goods and services

## KEY (CORRECT ANSWERS)

| | | | | |
|---|---|---|---|---|
| 1. B | 11. A | 21. D | 31. B | 41. C |
| 2. B | 12. C | 22. D | 32. C | 42. B |
| 3. C | 13. D | 23. E | 33. B | 43. E |
| 4. E | 14. C | 24. E | 34. A | 44. B |
| 5. E | 15. A | 25. B | 35. D | 45. E |
| 6. C | 16. A | 26. E | 36. A | 46. B |
| 7. A | 17. D | 27. B | 37. A | 47. E |
| 8. A | 18. A | 28. C | 38. D | 48. E |
| 9. B | 19. E | 29. C | 39. D | 49. B |
| 10. B | 20. B | 30. D | 40. A | 50. B |

# EXAMINATION SECTION
# TEST 1

DIRECTIONS: Each question or incomplete statement is followed by several suggested answers or completions. Select the one that BEST answers the question or completes the statement. *PRINT THE LETTER OF THE CORRECT ANSWER IN THE SPACE AT THE RIGHT.*

1. World trade is not based *solely* on gold because

    A. gold is too costly
    B. the value of gold is not fixed
    C. the value of gold fluctuates with market conditions
    D. gold is not liquid enough
    E. the world's supply of gold is limited

2. How was adjustment of international trade achieved under the gold standard? Through

    A. changes in currency valuation
    B. administrative controls
    C. changes in price levels
    D. a balance of payments
    E. exchange rates

3. The fiscal policy used to fight against inflation is *most likely* to be one that

    A. reduces government expenditures
    B. raises interest rates
    C. raises personal or corporate tax rates
    D. lowers the required reserve ratio
    E. increases government expenditures

4. Gross National Product is a measure of

    A. the net creation of new wealth resulting from the productive activity of the economy
    B. the market value of goods and services sold during the year
    C. prices
    D. production
    E. investment expenditures

5. What is Knut Wicksell's MAIN objection to the classical economists' view of market equilibrium?

    A. Supply does not create its own demand
    B. Savers cannot be induced to postpone consumption by raising interest rates
    C. Financial institutions are not fully responsive to market conditions
    D. Equilibrium cannot be achieved with a net leakage
    E. The result of market equilibrium is deflation

6. Metals were used as a medium of exchange for all the following reasons EXCEPT it

    A. is abundant      B. can be stored       C. is divisible
    D. is homogeneous   E. is valued for its beauty

7. What is meant by the phrase, "Full Employment"?

   A. The difference between the number of jobs available and the number of workers unemployed
   B. A zero unemployment rate
   C. The difference between the number of jobs available and the number of people who are out of the labor force
   D. Jobs for all people in the labor force
   E. The difference between the number of persons unemployed and the number of unfilled jobs

8. Which of the following is TRUE?

   A. The poor consume more than the rich
   B. The rich consume a larger proportion of their income than the poor
   C. The poor save a larger proportion of their income than the rich
   D. Consumption is a stable function of disposable personal income
   E. The rich and poor consume a nearly identical proportion of their incomes

9. What is the MAIN difference between "money" and "near-money"?

   A. Value
   B. Acceptability
   C. Convenience
   D. Amount
   E. Liability

10. How does the Federal Reserve System increase the money supply? By
    I. buying government bonds from the commercial banks
    II. selling government securities to the private sector
    III. lowering the rediscount rate of the central government
    IV. reducing the required reserve ratio of commercial banks
    V. increasing membership in the Federal Reserve System

    The CORRECT answer is:

    A. I, V
    B. I, III, IV
    C. II, III, IV
    D. II, IV
    E. II, IV, V

11. Why is a tax-cut during a recession more desirable than raising government expenditures. It

    A. helps alleviate some of the poverty in the private sector
    B. allows private citizens the choice of how to spend additional expenditures
    C. achieves full employment faster
    D. is a more straightfoward policy
    E. allows the government to sell securities to private persons

12. Inflation favors

    A. creditors
    B. employers
    C. pension recipients
    D. insurance recipients
    E. borrowers

13. Which of the following are TRUE of a tight-money policy? It
    I. leads to higher interest rates
    II. is aimed at shrinking the aggregate demand for final goods and services
    III. affects all industries
    IV. is a remedy for an economy moving toward recession
    V. is achieved by boosting the discount rate

    The CORRECT answer is:

    A. I, II
    B. II, III
    C. I, II, V
    D. III, IV
    E. III, IV, V

13.____

14. What is the MAIN objection to the stabilization policy which prevails in the United States? It

    A. does not guarantee full employment
    B. attempts to force the economy into a perennial recession
    C. is entirely a function of the Executive Department
    D. depends on Congress's responding to the needs for ad hoc fiscal changes
    E. overreacts to the economic cycles

14.____

15. Macroeconomic aspects of international trade arise because

    A. countries engage in commerce
    B. countries have different currencies
    C. not all countries are on the gold standard
    D. trade imbalances cause economic instability
    E. unemployment can be exported

15.____

16. When an American purchases foreign securities, it is called

    A. short-term credit
    B. long-term credit
    C. a capital export
    D. a capital import
    E. a long-term debit

16.____

17. The volume of international trade is enhanced by

    A. barter arrangements
    B. use of gold for payment
    C. use of an international currency for payment
    D. use of currency acceptable to all for payment
    E. use of legal tender for all payments

17.____

18. When the gold standard was in effect, countries achieved a balance of trade through

    A. a foreign trade multiplier
    B. hedging
    C. short-term credits
    D. the rate of exchange
    E. the gold-flow mechanism

18.____

19. Which of the following are considered triggering mechanisms for less than full-employment inflation? When
    I. powerful trade unions force employers to pay wage increases
    II. firms raise prices because of agreements with each other not to engage in price competition
    III. prices in weak industries do not decline as those in high-demand industries rise
    IV. a boom occurs in the business world
    V. the government imposes forced-saving controls on the economy

    The CORRECT answer is:

    A. I, II, III    B. II, IV    C. I, V
    D. II, III       E. I, II, V

20. The sum of retained earnings and depreciation of business is called

    A. Transfer Payments
    B. Net Investment
    C. Gross Business Savings
    D. Net Savings
    E. Disposable Income

21. Which of the following specialize in time deposits?
    I. Savings and Loan Associations
    II. Mutual Savings Banks
    III. Life Insurance Companies
    IV. Commercial Banks
    V. Commodity Banks

    The CORRECT answer is:

    A. I, II         B. I, II, III    C. II, IV
    D. IV, V         E. III, IV, V

22. All of the following are TRUE of inflation EXCEPT:

    A. Inflation is relative from a time and geographic perspective
    B. Inflation may occur during booms
    C. Seasonal changes in price levels cannot be described as inflationary
    D. Inflation is caused by rising prices
    E. Inflationary situations are usually open to interpretation

23. Which of the following are TRUE of the transactions motive for holding money?
    I. It is not without cost
    II. Both households and firms hold only the bare minimum amount which is needed
    III. Households are motivated to hold money because of unforeseen emergencies
    IV. The higher the interest rate, the smaller the demand for holding money
    V. Firms hold money because receiving revenue does not coincide in time with payments

    The CORRECT answer is:

    A. I, IV         B. I, III, V     C. I, II, V
    D. I, IV, V      E. I, III, IV

24. Macroeconomic Theory reflects a certain social philosophy because it is concerned with

    A. the prevention of large-scale unemployment
    B. economic loss
    C. the causes and effects of inflation
    D. the determination and significance of interest rates
    E. the theory of income for individual households

25. How does the "Swedish budget" achieve stabilization?
    By

    A. lowering the tax rates during recessions and raising the tax rates during booms
    B. providing that government stockpiles of materials should be purchased in periods of weak demand and then drawn upon when demand becomes very tight
    C. lowering the required reserve ratio during recessions and raising it during inflationary periods
    D. increasing government expenditures during recessions and cutting back expenditures during inflations
    E. maintaining policies which will keep the changing levels of investment from severely disturbing the economy

26. What is the MAIN difference between a pegged exchange rate and a flexible exchange rate? The MAIN difference lies in how

    A. the exchange rate is determined
    B. credit is extended
    C. gold is exchanged
    D. adjustment to market conditions is achieved
    E. the external price of currency is measured

27. What is the role of the International Monetary Fund?
    To

    A. extend credit
    B. fix exchange rates
    C. impose controls on movements of commodities and capital
    D. facilitate international trade
    E. prevent another worldwide depression

28. Which factor affects the level of investment the MOST?

    A. Rate of interest
    B. Expectations of entrepreneurs
    C. Technological innovations
    D. Taxation
    E. Wage rate

29. When a business boom causes an inflation, it is limited by the

    A. gap between excess demand over supply
    B. interest rate
    C. limited creation of high-powered money
    D. tax increases
    E. velocity of money

30. The commercial banking system is **never** fully loaned-up because

    A. of legal reserve requirements
    B. money leaks out of the system
    C. money cannot be created
    D. of the amount of currency held by the public
    E. there are too many separate banks

31. Which of the following are TRUE of money? Money is
    I. necessary to continue to produce and exchange real commodities
    II. necessary to produce and consume as much as we currently do
    III. necessary for the functioning of a modern economy
    IV. essential to the process of exchange in a modern economy
    V. the only commodity that serves as a store of value

    The CORRECT answer is:

    A. I, III, V            B. I, II, III, IV          C. III, V
    D. II, III, IV          E. All of the above

32. What causes the supply of money to change in a commercial banking system? The

    A. excess reserve situation
    B. amount of currency in circulation
    C. amount of currency held by the public
    D. number of banking branches
    E. number of loans issued

33. The Keynesian "liquidity trap" is **LEAST likely** to occur when

    A. the Federal Reserve System publicizes use of the discount rate tool
    B. a monetary policy is not applied at the outset of the recession
    C. the recession is severe
    D. the recession is mild
    E. firms expect prices to continue to fall

34. Which of the following are TRUE of hyperinflation? It
    I. is characterized by a mild but steady rise in the general price level
    II. occurs when the government creates far too much money
    III. causes households and firms to hold too much money
    IV. causes the purchasing power of money to decline
    V. decreases the velocity of money

    The CORRECT answer is :

    A. I, II, IV            B. I, II, V               C. II, III
    D. II, IV               E. II, III, V

35. Which economic situation is most readily solved with better functioning product and factor markets in terms of reducing imperfections and barriers to price competition?

    A. Hyperinflation              B. Repressed inflation
    C. Demand-pull inflation       D. Structural demand inflation
    E. Cost-push inflation

36. When a nation devalues its currency, it hopes to

    A. *increase* exports
    B. *increase* imports
    C. *affect* the price of gold
    D. *increase* its purchasing power
    E. *raise* the general price level

37. Which of the following are arguments in favor of a flexible exchange rate? It
    I. *allows* nations to hold the exchange rates stable and to help others to do so
    II. *frees* governments from having to hold huge amounts of foreign currencies to finance deficits
    III. *does not require* trade restrictions to curtail the net outflow of gold
    IV. *eliminates* speculative movements of capital before and after devaluation
    V. *does not add* to the uncertainty factor in business

    The CORRECT answer is:

    A. I, V
    B. I, IV, V
    C. II, III, IV
    D. II, IV
    E. III, V

38. The monetarist or traditional approach contends that the stock of money and changes in it cause

    A. a state of full employment
    B. the shocks in the American economy
    C. built-in stabilizers to operate automatically
    D. optimism in the business and financial communities
    E. short-term stabilization

39. Why is a counter-inflationary monetary policy LESS desirable than a restrictive fiscal policy? It

    A. results in a greater likelihood that the liquidity trap will occur
    B. may generate pessimism in the business and financial communities
    C. affects the marginal propensity to consume
    D. results in a cutback of government expenditures
    E. stifles one or two industries in order to cure the entire economy

40. What is the aim of the fiscal policy of cutting back taxes during a recession? To

    A. *increase* the budgetary deficit
    B. *balance* the budget
    C. *restore* full employment to the economy
    D. *increase* consumption
    E. *increase* the reserves of commercial banks

41. All of the following are components of "near money" EXCEPT

    A. U.S. bonds
    B. short-term debt
    C. the cash value of insurance policies
    D. time deposits
    E. demand deposits

8 (#1)

42. Which of the following are built-in stabilizers in the economy?
    I. Unemployment insurance payments
    II. Open market operations
    III. Private pensions and social security benefits
    IV. Tax reductions
    V. Dividend payments to stockholders
    The CORRECT answer is:

    A. I, II, III
    D. II, IV
    B. I, III
    E. I, III, IV
    C. I, III, V

43. What causes cost-push inflation?

    A. Technological advances which trigger a business boom
    B. Full employment
    C. Firms raising prices to counter rising costs
    D. Government stockpiles of materials
    E. Some components of the prime index rise while others remain stationary

44. Which of the following are VALID arguments against opponents to a federal debt?
    I. Businesses finance themselves through debt
    II. The overwhelming portion of the debt is of recent origin
    III. Stabilization policies imply deficits, planned balances, or surpluses
    IV. Most of the federal debt is held by foreigners
    V. More capital investment in the present leads to higher output in the future
    The CORRECT answer is:

    A. I, III, IV
    D. III, IV
    B. II, V
    E. I, II, V
    C. I, III, V

45. What is the main disadvantage of the stabilization policy of "formula flexibility"? It

    A. cannot guarantee a state of full employment
    B. can overreact to the economic cycles and accelerate or decelerate the stock of money erroneously
    C. sets artificial boundaries for the rate of increase of the money stock
    D. leads to automatic increases or reductions of tax rates which are, sometimes, based on an index reflecting changes in irrelevant factors
    E. depends on legislation that may be enacted too late or which may be completely absent

46. What does a "balance of payments deficit" refer to?

    A. A transaction that requires foreign currency
    B. A transaction that increases the supply of foreign currency
    C. An account indicating American imports exceed exports
    D. A situation where returns on capital abroad are higher than in the United States
    E. The balance of payments without the balancing items

47. What was the MAIN contribution John Maynard Keynes made to economics? His

    A. understanding of aggregate demand
    B. criticism of classical and neo-classical economists
    C. theory of how a modern economic system operates

D. ability to demonstrate the self-correcting mechanisms in the economy
E. application of laissez-faire to modern economic theory

48. What is "hard currency"? Money that

   A. is acceptable to other countries in international exchanges between them
   B. is backed by gold
   C. Is full-bodied
   D. cannot be devaluated
   E. is loaned by the International Monetary Fund

49. What is the result of the condition in which the economy suffers from a "fiscal drag"?

   A. There has been a secular decline in the ratio of federal debt to GNP
   B. The percentage in tax collection exceeds the percentage growth of the GNP
   C. The price index falls below a certain critical point
   D. Economic instability is aggravated by the lag of legislative action
   E. Decelerations in the stock of money cause downswings in economic activities

50. A tight money policy particularly discriminates against

   A. investment in residential construction
   B. investment in the business community
   C. long-term loans
   D. government expenditures
   E. firms competing with households

## KEY (CORRECT ANSWERS)

| | | | | |
|---|---|---|---|---|
| 1. E | 11. B | 21. C | 31. D | 41. E |
| 2. C | 12. E | 22. D | 32. A | 42. C |
| 3. C | 13. C | 23. C | 33. D | 43. C |
| 4. D | 14. D | 24. A | 34. D | 44. C |
| 5. C | 15. B | 25. A | 35. E | 45. D |
| 6. A | 16. D | 26. D | 36. A | 46. E |
| 7. A | 17. D | 27. D | 37. C | 47. C |
| 8. D | 18. E | 28. A | 38. B | 48. A |
| 9. C | 19. A | 29. C | 39. E | 49. B |
| 10. B | 20. C | 30. B | 40. D | 50. A |

# EXAMINATION SECTION
# TEST 1

DIRECTIONS: Each question or incomplete statement is followed by several suggested answers or completions. Select the one that BEST answers the question or completes the statement. *PRINT THE LETTER OF THE CORRECT ANSWER IN THE SPACE AT THE RIGHT.*

1. HOW DOES a country solve a balance-of-payments deficit under a Pegged Exchange Rate System? By
    I. *borrowing* from the International Monetary Fund
    II. *floating* long-term securities
    III. *raising* the price of foreign currency
    IV. *changing* the exchange rate in the market
    V. *converting* domestic securities into investment in all kinds of foreign securities

    The CORRECT answer is:

    A. I, II, IV
    B. I, III
    C. I, IV
    D. I, III, IV
    E. I, IV, V

1.____

2. WHAT is the purpose of a Price Index? It

    A. *indicates* price changes in any one given year
    B. *lists* the prices of goods and services in any one given year
    C. *summarizes* the average price of a group of goods and services in a onetime period relative to another
    D. *measures* the current dollar value of the GNP
    E. *points up* inflationary and recessionary tendencies within the economy

2.____

3. WHICH of the following BEST explains the growth of production in the United States?

    A. Growth of the population
    B. Increases in the factors of production
    C. Increases in the average educational levels of the labor force
    D. Increases in the supply of money
    E. Technological change

3.____

4. WHICH of the following are determinants of the demand for capital by business? The
    I. present amount of money held by the firm
    II. expected stream of future income
    III. price of capital goods
    IV. current rate of interest
    V. present indebtedness

    The CORRECT answer is:

    A. I, III, V
    B. II, III, IV
    C. I, IV, V
    D. II, IV, V
    E. All of the above

4.____

5. WHAT is the MOST unstable component of aggregate demand? _____ demand.

    A. Consumption
    B. Investment
    C. Induced
    D. Government
    E. Export

5.____

41

6. WHAT causes reduction in purchasing power of income or wealth during an inflation?

   A. Constant salaries
   B. Increase in prices
   C. Increase in unemployment
   D. Increase in price per unit of a product
   E. Decrease in disposable income

7. All of the following are TRUE of the Price System EXCEPT: It

   A. leads to an efficient allocation of resources
   B. leads to an unequal distribution of income
   C. ensures continued employment of labor and other resources
   D. allows firms to grow large enough to restrict output and raise prices
   E. reveals that prices often reflect only private rather than social costs and benefits

8. WHICH of the following are included in this year's GNP? A
   I. car manufactured this year but not yet sold
   II. car manufactured and sold this year
   III. car manufactured last year and sold this year
   IV. Used car sold this year
   V. used car that is rebuilt and painted this year

   The CORRECT answer is:

   A. I, II         B. I, II, V        C. II, III, IV
   D. II, III, IV, V    E. All of the above

9. A marginal propensity to consume of 0.60 indicates that

   A. a household will consume 0.40 of any decrease in its level of disposable income
   B. a household will consume 0.40 regardless of the level of disposable income
   C. a household consumes 0.60 of its level of disposable income
   D. a household will consume 0.60 of any increase in its level of disposable income
   E. None of the above

10. Inflationary pressures are relieved by

    A. an increase in taxes
    B. an increase in taxes and government spending
    C. a decrease in taxes
    D. a decrease in taxes and government spending
    E. reducing the public debt

11. WHAT is the aim of the United States' economic policy? To eliminate _____ unemployment.

    A. frictional       B. cyclical        C. structural
    D. seasonal         E. all

12. A variation in business or economic activity which takes place within a one-year period, describes

    A. a secular trend              B. a business cycle
    C. a seasonal fluctuation       D. creeping inflation
    E. cost-push inflation

13. All of the following are *PRINCIPAL* Summary National Income Accounts except

    A. National Income
    B. Gross National Product
    C. Gross Investment
    D. Net National Product
    E. Personal Income

14. *WHICH* of the following are functions of money? A
    I. medium of exchange
    II. commodity standard
    III. standard of value
    IV. determinant of price levels
    V. store of value

    The *CORRECT* answer is:

    A. I, II
    B. I, III, V
    C. I, II, III
    D. I, III, IV
    E. All of the above

15. In the rigid version of the Quantity Theory of Money, changes in

    A. velocity are proportional to changes in the money supply
    B. the nominal GNP are proportional to changes in the money supply
    C. the nominal GNP are proportional to changes in velocity
    D. the price level are proportional to changes in the money supply
    E. the price level are controlled by the money supply

16. *WHY* do demand deposits account for over 90% of all money transactions in the United States? A demand deposit is

    A. a bearer instrument
    B. more convenient
    C. interest-bearing
    D. a safer way of holding money
    E. a more acceptable means of exchange

17. *WHY* will a commercial bank hold excess reserves? To
    I. maintain solvency
    II. meet unexpected currency demands
    III. satisfy possible reserve losses resulting from the transfer of deposits to competing commercial banks
    IV. anticipate the future loan demands of borrowers
    V. comply with requirements of the Federal Open Market Committee

    The *CORRECT* answer is:

    A. I, II, III
    B. I, II, V
    C. II, III, IV
    D. I, III, V
    E. All of the above

18. According to Monetarists, changes in the money supply

    A. shift the demand-for-money schedule
    B. have no effect on the quantity of money demanded
    C. have an effect only upon household spending
    D. have a highly variable effect upon the level of income
    E. have an effect upon consumption and investment spending

19. WHAT is the KEY element in the growth process of an economy? Increase in the

   A. quantity and quality of natural resources
   B. economy's population
   C. population's participation in the labor force
   D. quality of labor
   E. accumulation of capital

20. Measures used to restore equilibrium in the balance of payments can have the effect of

   A. promoting international liquidity
   B. aggravating an unemployment problem
   C. reducing gold supplies
   D. reducing international reserves
   E. lowering the interest rate

21. WHICH of the following are counted as part of the GNP?
   I. Wheat grown and sold by farmers
   II. Flour sold by the mill to bakers
   III. Bread produced by bakers and sold to supermarkets
   IV. Bread sold to the ultimate consumer
   V. Bread sold to commercial sandwich makers
   The CORRECT answer is:

   A. I, III, IV            B. I, II, III            C. III, IV, V
   D. IV, V                 E. All of the above

22. What is "real GNP"?

   A. A measure of the volume of real goods and services produced independently of price changes
   B. The market value of all goods and services
   C. The measure of the aggregate productive performance of the economy
   D. The average price of goods and services in one time-period relative to another
   E. The total income earned in the society

23. WHICH of the following is(are) part of the productive process?
   I. Extraction of raw materials
   II. Manufacture of intermediate products
   III. Assembly of final goods
   IV. Wholesaling activities
   V. Retailing activities
   The CORRECT answer is:

   A. I, II, III            B. III only              C. I, III, V
   D. III, IV, V            E. All of the above

24. WHAT is the relationship among the components of production, income, and demand, in a demand model?

   A. Interdependent        B. Equal                 C. Autonomous
   D. Dependent             E. Cumulative

5 (#1)

25. Government demand depends PRIMARILY on

    A. the size of production
    B. the price of social capital
    C. the current rate of interest
    D. military commitments abroad
    E. how society's desire for public goods is represented in the political process

26. WHICH of the following equations is CORRECT?

    A. GNI = GNP
    B. GNI ≠ GNP
    C. GNI > GNP
    D. GNI < GNP
    E. GNP - GNI = Production

27. WHICH of the following events will NOT cause the market demand curve to shift upward?

    A. Increase in the number of consumers
    B. Increase in consumers' income
    C. Prices of substitute commodities rise
    D. Prices of complementary commodities rise
    E. Consumers' taste for the commodity increase

28. HOW does Current Dollar GNP differ from Constant Dollar GNP?

    A. It measures GNP in current year prices
    B. It measures GNP in base year prices
    C. It measures GNP during the current year
    D. It measures GNP during a one-year period
    E. There is no difference

29. WHAT does Say's Law conclude about the employment of economic resources?

    A. Full employment of economic resources is the normal condition of a private enterprise system
    B. The goal of a private enterprise economy is full employment of economic resources
    C. Full employment of economic resources can never occur in a private enterprise economy
    D. Full employment of economic resources is dependent upon production in a private enterprise economy
    E. Full employment of economic resources will approach, but never equal, the production level of a private enterprise economy

30. WHICH of the following is an example of discretionary fiscal policy?

    A. Government welfare payments
    B. Employer pension plans
    C. Payment of unemployment insurance
    D. Automatic changes in gross tax receipts that result from the income tax structure
    E. Deliberate changes in the level of government spending and net tax receipts

31. The contraction phase of the business cycle is characterized by

    A. *falling* interest rates
    B. *falling* price levels

C. *falling* unemployment levels
D. *rising* interest rates
E. *rising* economic activity

32. Frictional unemployment generally occurs

    A. in a government-controlled society
    B. in a changing, free society
    C. in an economy experiencing technological advance
    D. during periods of insufficient aggregate demand
    E. in industries that are highly unionized

33. WHICH of the following is TRUE during a recession? _____ are severely affected.

    A. Non-durable goods
    B. Capital goods
    C. Durable goods
    D. Non-durable and durable goods
    E. Capital and durable goods

34. WHAT is the relationship between Net Investment and Gross Investment?

    A. Net Investment equals Gross Investment less taxes
    B. Net Investment equals Gross Investment less depreciation
    C. Net Investment equals Gross Investment less savings
    D. Net Investment equals Gross Investment less payments to the factors of production
    E. Net Investment equals Gross Investment less consumption

35. WHAT is the $M_1$ definition of money in the USA?
    I. Paper currency
    II. Demand deposits
    III. Deposits at non-bank thrift institutions
    IV. Time deposits at commercial banks
    V. Savings deposits at commercial banks

    The CORRECT answer is:

    A. I, V
    B. I, IV, V
    C. I, II
    D. I, II, V
    E. All of the above

36. WHICH of the following may be considered a monetary standard?
    I. Paper currency
    II. Coins
    III. Gold
    IV. Silver
    V. Government securities

    The CORRECT answer is:

    A. I, II, V
    B. II, III, V
    C. II, III, IV
    D. I, V
    E. All of the above

7 (#1)

37. WHAT are the commercial banks' *PRINCIPAL* sources of liquidity?   37._____
    I. Currency
    II. Deposits at the Federal Reserve
    III. Money-market instruments
    IV. Short-and long-term loans to customers
    V. Fixed income obligations

    The *CORRECT* answer is:

    A. I, II, III          B. I, II                C. II, III, V
    D. I, II, IV           E. All of the above

38. *WHICH* of the following is TRUE of the National Income Theory? It   38._____
    A. focuses upon the expansion of aggregate supply over time
    B. evaluates the effect of resource growth upon productive capacity
    C. evaluates the increase in individuals' standard of living
    D. evaluates the rate at which aggregate demand must increase to achieve maximum growth
    E. has as its objective the design of economic policies that will move the economy onto the production possibility curve

39. Classical economists restore equilibrium to the world market by relying on   39._____
    A. changes in the rate of exchange
    B. devaluation of currencies
    C. the foreign-trade multiplier
    D. absolutely flexible price levels
    E. changing interest rates

40. *WHY* are intermediate products NOT counted as part of the GNP? They   40._____
    A. are an insignificant part of total productive activity
    B. would overestimate productive activity
    C. are goods that never reach the ultimate consumer
    D. are not considered part of the market value of goods and services
    E. might become part of a final product

41. Capital, as a factor of production, includes   41._____
    I. stocks and bonds
    II. currency
    III. machines
    IV. buildings
    V. inventories

    The *CORRECT* answer is:

    A. I, II               B. I, III, IV, V         C. I, II, V
    D. III, IV, V          E. All of the above

42. *WHAT* is the MAIN problem in constructing a price index?   42._____
    A. Data is difficult to obtain
    B. Prices of some units have risen while those for others have fallen
    C. There is no set averaging procedure that takes into account the relative importance of goods and services

D. The set of goods and services, to which the average price has to be compared at different times, is constantly changing
E. Prices are a function of the economy at specific times and cannot easily be compared because of variations in the economy

43. WHAT is the difference between a consumption good and an investment good? The   43._____

    A. source of the demand for the good
    B. type of good
    C. durability of the good
    D. degree of demand for the good
    E. production factor of the good

44. WHAT determines the marginal efficiency of capital for business? The   44._____

    A. current rate of interest
    B. rate of depreciation
    C. income stream and the price of capital goods
    D. rate of interest and the price of capital goods
    E. opportunity cost

45. All of the following items determine consumption demand EXCEPT   45._____

    A. expected future income
    B. disposable income
    C. population
    D. recent standard of living
    E. interest rates

46. WHERE is the real impact of inflation? On the   46._____

    A. level of real income
    B. level of disposable income
    C. level of price increases
    D. distribution level of income
    E. value of money

47. A demand schedule shows the relationship between the quantity demanded of a commodity over a given period of time AND the   47._____

    A. taste of consumers
    B. money income of consumers
    C. price of related products
    D. price of the commodity
    E. supply available

48. WHAT is the disposable income of a person whose personal income is $15,000, with personal income taxes of $3200, consumption at $7500, interest and payments amounting to $280, and personal savings totaling $4020?   48._____

    A. $15,000        B. $11,520        C. $4020
    D. $11,800        E. $4300

49. WHICH of the following is NOT a component of aggregate spending?   49._____

    A. Gross private domestic investment
    B. Personal consumption expenditures
    C. Government transfers
    D. Government purchase of goods and services
    E. Net exports

50. The ratio of the change in saving to the change in disposable income is called the   50._____

    A. consumption function
    B. average propensity to save
    C. average propensity to consume
    D. marginal propensity to save
    E. marginal propensity to consume

## KEY (CORRECT ANSWERS)

| | | | | |
|---|---|---|---|---|
| 1. B | 11. B | 21. D | 31. A | 41. D |
| 2. C | 12. C | 22. A | 32. B | 42. D |
| 3. E | 13. C | 23. E | 33. E | 43. C |
| 4. B | 14. B | 24. A | 34. B | 44. C |
| 5. B | 15. D | 25. E | 35. C | 45. A |
| 6. D | 16. D | 26. A | 36. E | 46. D |
| 7. C | 17. C | 27. D | 37. A | 47. D |
| 8. B | 18. E | 28. A | 38. E | 48. D |
| 9. D | 19. E | 29. A | 39. D | 49. C |
| 10. A | 20. B | 30. E | 40. B | 50. D |

# EXAMINATION SECTION
# TEST 1

DIRECTIONS: Each question or incomplete statement is followed by several suggested answers or completions. Select the one that BEST answers the question or completes the statement. *PRINT THE LETTER OF THE CORRECT ANSWER IN THE SPACE AT THE RIGHT.*

1. What does the statement that the GNP rose between 1998 and 2009 by $485.0 billions, or 108%, actually mean?   1.____

    A. The market value of final goods produced in 2009 was 108% greater than in 1998
    B. There were 108% more goods and services produced in 2009 than in 1998
    C. Society was 108% better off in 2009 than in 1998
    D. The market value of goods produced in 2009 was 108% greater than the market value of goods produced in 1998
    E. It means that market prices increased by 108% over the twelve-year period

2. *HOW* does GNP compare with GNI in a given year?   2.____

    A. GNP is always higher
    B. GNP is always lower
    C. GNP equals GNI
    D. GNP is GNI
    E. They cannot be compared without more data

3. *WHAT* determines disposable income?   3.____

    A. Savings        B. Production        C. Income
    D. Interest rates E. Demand

4. The demand of businesses for new capital that does NOT include new capital replacing depreciated capital, is called _____ investment.   4.____

    A. opportunity    B. capital           C. optimum
    D. gross          E. net

5. *WHICH* of the following are examples of non-durable goods demanded by households?   5.____
    I. Sporting equipment
    II. Clothing
    III. Transportation
    IV. Food and beverages
    V. Water

    The *CORRECT* answer is:

    A. I, II          B. I, IV, V          C. III, V
    D. II, IV         E. IV, V

6. Demand-pull inflation develops when economic resources are fully employed *AND* there is a(n)   6.____
    I. increase in aggregate demand
    II. rise in business taxes which results in higher costs
    III. shortage of specific labor skills or supplies prior to full employment
    IV. surplus of materials which raises prices that are passed on to the consumer
    V. aggregate demand which grows at a faster rate than aggregate supply

51

The CORRECT answer is:

A. I, V  B. I, III, V  C. II, III, IV
D. II, IV  E. I, II, V

7. During a period of stable prices, one would expect

   A. high unemployment
   B. low unemployment
   C. greater aggregate demand
   D. lower aggregate demand
   E. economic equilibrium

8. WHICH of the following are examples of indirect business taxes?
   I. Excise taxes
   II. Sales taxes
   III. Business property taxes
   IV. Import duties
   V. License fees

   The CORRECT answer is:

   A. I, II  B. II, IV  C. I, III, V
   D. III, V  E. All of the above

9. WHAT is the objective of changes in government spending and taxes? To

   A. balance the budget
   B. prevent inflations and recessions
   C. promote maximum employment, productivity, and purchasing power
   D. guarantee a basic standard of living to all citizens
   E. satisfy the public debt

10. When workers are between jobs or in the process of changing jobs, it is termed _____ unemployment.

    A. seasonal  B. short-term  C. structural
    D. frictional  E. cyclical

11. What distinguishes hyperinflation from other forms of inflation?

    A. There is a reduction in the purchasing power of a unit of money
    B. Real income and wealth are affected
    C. The results are not shared equally by all economic groups
    D. There are annual increases in the general price level
    E. There is no dependable monetary system available to facilitate exchange

12. WHICH of the following is NOT included in the National Income?

    A. Wages  B. Rent  C. Interest
    D. Depreciation  E. Profit

13. When money serves as a standard of value, it is akin to

    I. the speed of sound and night
    II. the value of gold and silver
    III. the weight and size of objects
    IV. the calories found in foods
    V. liquid assets

    The CORRECT answer is:

    A. I, IV
    B. II, V
    C. I, III, IV
    D. I, III, IV, V
    E. All of the above

14. WHICH of the following represent a Monetarist viewpoint?

    I. Money is unique
    II. The demandr formoney is sensitive to the rate of interest
    III. The velocity of money is variable
    IV. Fiscal measures result in only a small net change in the level of income
    V. Discretionary monetary management is a stabilizing factor in the economy

    The CORRECT answer is:

    A. I, IV, V
    B. II, III, IV
    C. I, II, IV
    D. II, III, V
    E. II, III, IV, V

15. WHICH of the following is not a MAJOR source of increased productive capacity?

    A. The quantity and quality of natural resources
    B. An increase in the population's participation in the labor force
    C. An increase in the number of hours worked by the labor force
    D. An increase in the accumulation of capital
    E. Advances in technology

16. Why does the current IMF system perpetuate balance-of-payment maladjustments? Because of

    A. inflexible price levels
    B. economic goals of modern countries in full employment
    C. the inflexible exchange rate
    D. ill-defined terms of trade
    E. speculations in foreign currencies

17. Production in the United States economy does NOT include

    I. illegal goods
    II. services of housewives
    III. householders owning their own homes
    IV. the value of food produced and consumed on farms
    V. the value of food produced and consumed by household gardeners

    The CORRECT answer is:

    A. I, II
    B. I, II, V
    C. II, III, V
    D. I, II, III, V
    E. All of the above

18. WHAT does the future stream of income for businesses depend on? Expected
    I. levels of future demand
    II. cost reductions from using capital
    III. levels of production
    IV. levels of investment
    V. technological change

    The CORRECT answer is:

    A. I, III, IV
    B. I, IV, V
    C. I, III
    D. I, II, V
    E. I, III, IV, V

19. Aggregate demand is equal to the sum of all of the following demands EXCEPT

    A. consumption
    B. investment
    C. government
    D. export
    E. import

20. The amount of wages, interest, and rent required to hire one unit of labor, capital, or land is called the

    A. real output
    B. price mechanism
    C. factor price
    D. production price
    E. substitution effect

21. WHICH of the following is a CORRECT assumption based on Say's Law? Individuals

    A. work to satisfy non-economic desires
    B. work to buy goods and services
    C. work to create and add to a "nest-egg"
    D. consume beyond their disposable income
    E. consume at a rate equal to their disposable income

22. HOW can an inflationary gap be eliminated? By

    A. an increase in government spending and a decrease in net tax revenues
    B. equal decreases in net tax revenues and government spending
    C. equal increases in net tax revenues and government spending
    D. decreases in net tax revenues
    E. an increase in net tax revenues and a decrease in transfer payments

23. WHAT does the "Potential GNP" measure?

    A. How much could be produced when land, labor, and capital are fully utilized
    B. Next year's output based on economic trends indicated by this year's GNP
    C. Output at full employment
    D. Output when 100% of the civilian labor force is employed
    E. Output when the economy is at equilibrium

24. An expansion period in the business cycle is characterized by increases in
    I. employment
    II. prices
    III. money supply
    IV. interest
    V. profits

    The CORRECT answer is:

    A. I, III
    B. II, III, V
    C. I, III
    D. I, II, III, V
    E. All of the above

25. The average number of times a unit of money is used during the year to purchase final goods and services, is called the  25.____

    A. rate of exchange
    B. store of value
    C. velocity of money
    D. common denominator
    E. demand factor

26. When a country adopts a commodity standard, the money supply depends upon the  26.____
    I. promissory notes issued by the government
    II. aggregate demand for the chosen commodity
    III. defined commodity content of the paper currency
    IV. available quantity of the chosen commodity
    V. commercial use of the commodity

    The CORRECT answer is:

    A. I, II, III            B. II, III, IV, V        C. I, II, III, IV
    D. III, IV, V            E. III, IV

27. All of the following are TRUE of the Monetarists EXCEPT:  27.____

    A. Monetarists favor stable monetary growth rather than discretionary monetary management
    B. Monetarists view monetary policy as a means to achieving a more efficient allocation of resources
    C. Monetarists contend that monetary policy is predictable due to the sensitivity of velocity to the rate of interest
    D. Monetarists contend that monetary policy crowds out private investment
    E. Monetarists contend that velocity is predictable

28. An economy's poverty level is relative to the economy's  28.____

    A. resources
    B. capital
    C. population growth
    D. standard of living
    E. per capita output

29. All of the following are changes in the structure of the economy which guarantee a higher degree of stability EXCEPT:  29.____

    A. The flow of government expenditures is stable
    B. Disposable personal income fluctuations are reduced
    C. Deposits in banks are federally insured
    D. The Federal Reserve System prevents the collapse of banks
    E. The public has greater confidence in the economy

30. The level of production tends to adjust to  30.____

    A. price levels
    B. the factors of production available
    C. the level of aggregate demand
    D. the highest profit margin
    E. the rate of production

31. When should a product be demanded by the government? When

    A. it benefits the public sector
    B. its value outweighs its cost
    C. it benefits the private sector
    D. it ensures production of goods
    E. the interest rate declines

32. WHAT is the largest component of aggregate demand? _____ demand.

    A. Consumption      B. Investment      C. Induced
    D. Government       E. Export

33. WHAT is wealth?

    A. The assets that result from economic activity
    B. An accumulated stock of material assets
    C. Income minus expenditures
    D. Resources
    E. Anything of market value

34. WHICH of the following does NOT cause an increase in supply? A(n)

    A. increase in the number of producers of the commodity
    B. reduction in the price of other commodities related in production
    C. reduction in factor prices
    D. improvement in technology
    E. increase in the commodity price

35. The business sector's ability to produce does NOT depend on

    A. the quantity of economic resources supplied by the household sector
    B. the quantity of labor units
    C. the amount of capital available
    D. natural resources
    E. the ability to sell output

36. WHICH of the following is TRUE of the public debt? It

    A. burdens future generations
    B. eventually will lead to Federal bankruptcy
    C. aggravates inflationary and recessionary tendencies
    D. burdens individuals who elect to save and not consume
    E. burdens individuals who elect to consume and not save

37. The Accelerator Theory is used to explain

    A. the business cycle
    B. how changes in investment affect the business cycle
    C. fluctuations in capital stock and the level of inventory investment
    D. fluctuations in capital stock and technological change
    E. fluctuations in inventories over the business cycle

38. According to the Acceleration Principle, net investment is a constant sum each year when sales

   A. volume decreases
   B. volume remains constant
   C. Increase by a decreasing sum each year
   D. increase by a constant sum each year
   E. increase at a constant rate each year

38.____

39. WHY are financial assets, other than money, NOT accepted as a medium of exchange?

   A. They are not safe
   B. They lose nominal value when converted into money
   C. They do not have a fixed nominal value
   D. They must first be converted into money-..
   E. They are not readily converted into money

39.____

40. The Federal Reserve System consists of
   I. a Board of Governors
   II. a Monetary Fund Committee
   III. Member commercial banks
   IV. Member Savings and Loan Associations
   V. District Federal Reserve Banks
   The CORRECT answer is:

   A. I, II, V
   B. I, III, V
   C. I, II, III, V
   D. II, III, IV, V
   E. All of the above

40.____

41. According to the Phillips Curve, high unemployment rates are associated with

   A. low rates of inflation
   B. high rates of inflation
   C. large increases in wages
   D. small increases in wages
   E. low productive rates

41.____

42. All of the following are objections to economic growth EXCEPT: It

   A. pollutes the atmosphere
   B. does not resolve socio-economic problems
   C. eliminates the need for substitute goods
   D. wastes economic resources
   E. leads to man's enslavement by technology

42.____

43. WHEN is income in equilibrium? When

   A. consumption and saving are equal
   B. consumption and disposable income are equal
   C. intended investment and savings are equal
   D. all disposable income is consumed
   E. the marginal propensity to save is equal to the marginal propensity to consume

43.____

44. The aggregate demand for goods and services produced in the economy equals total demand

    A. *less* autonomous demand
    B. *plus* export demand
    C. *less* export demand
    D. *plus* import demand
    E. *less* import demand

45. *WHAT* is the average propensity to save for an individual whose yearly disposable income is $50,000 and consumption is $46,000?

    A. 0.80   B. 1.08   C. 0.92   D. 0.08   E. 0.90

46. *WHAT* is Cyclical Unemployment? Unemployment

    A. caused by insufficient aggregate demand
    B. due to changes in demand for particular products
    C. caused by technological advance
    D. due to workers being temporarily out of work
    E. due to workers voluntarily leaving the job market

47. *WHAT* category of unemployment describes a worker who lacks the skills needed to qualify for available job openings? unemployment.

    A. Frictional      B. Productive      C. Structural
    D. Cyclical        E. Linear

48. An inconvertible paper standard consists of a money supply that

    A. is backed by gold
    B. is backed by gold but is not convertible into gold
    C. is backed by a specific commodity but is not convertible into that commodity
    D. includes only the debts of commercial banks which have gold backing
    E. includes the debts of the government and/or commercial banks

49. The number of district Federal Reserve Banks is

    A. 6   B. 12   C. 18   D. 24   E. 36

50. Keynesian Theory emphasizes the use of

    A. monetary policy
    B. fiscal policy
    C. open market valuations
    D. selective credit controls
    E. reserve requirements

## KEY (CORRECT ANSWERS)

| | | | | |
|---|---|---|---|---|
| 1. D | 11. E | 21. B | 31. B | 41. A |
| 2. C | 12. D | 22. B | 32. A | 42. C |
| 3. B | 13. C | 23. C | 33. B | 43. C |
| 4. E | 14. C | 24. E | 34. E | 44. E |
| 5. D | 15. A | 25. C | 35. E | 45. D |
| 6. B | 16. C | 26. D | 36. D | 46. A |
| 7. A | 17. B | 27. D | 37. E | 47. C |
| 8. E | 18. D | 28. D | 38. D | 48. E |
| 9. C | 19. E | 29. D | 39. D | 49. B |
| 10. D | 20. C | 30. C | 40. B | 50. B |

# EXAMINATION SECTION
## TEST 1

DIRECTIONS: Each question or incomplete statement is followed by several suggested answers or completions. Select the one that BEST answers the question or completes the statement. *PRINT THE LETTER OF THE CORRECT ANSWER IN THE SPACE AT THE RIGHT.*

1. Economists who believe in the equilibrium theory of unemployment would be LEAST likely to place a major share of blame for unemployment on

    A. monetary conditions
    B. maldistribution of economic resources
    C. lack of mobility of labor
    D. government floors under prices and wages

    1.____

2. Which one of the social functions listed below do interest and land rent perform? They

    A. act to withdraw resources from use in present consumption
    B. serve to direct their respective factors of production into the most valuable and useful channels
    C. stimulate increased supply of their respective factors
    D. help to maintain balance between the provision for present and future wants

    2.____

3. Review of interest rates in specific countries over long periods of time reveals long-term trends of

    A. constancy, that can most reasonably be explained in terms of persistent traits of human psychology
    B. variability, that can be most correctly associated with changes in the productivity of capital
    C. variability, that can be most correctly associated with cyclical fluctuations in the economy
    D. constancy, that can most reasonably be explained in terms of consistent superiority of capitalistic methods of production over the techniques of less developed economies

    3.____

4. Which of the following are CORRECT statements of modern economic theory as related to profit?
    I. Pure profit tends to disappear as a state of balanced competition is approached.
    II. Pure profit results from the imperfections of competition.
    III. Pure profit is the net income of a business as a whole, rather than the return for entrepreneurial service.
    IV. Scientific management and insurance have minimized the validity of the concept of profit as *compensation for risk-taking*.

    The CORRECT answer is:

    A. I, II, III, IV   B. I, II
    C. III, IV          D. I, III

    4.____

5. Study of United States corporate financing practices during the period after World War II indicates more financing by

   A. bond issues than by stock issues, partly due to the tax advantage involved in bond financing
   B. stock issues than by bond issues, partly due to the advantage involved in stock financing
   C. stock issues than by bond issues, due to the shortage of equity capital
   D. bond issues than by stock issues, due to the shortage of equity capital

6. Which one of the following statements concerning the control of monetary and credit conditions in the United States is NOT correct?

   A. The fact that the Federal Reserve Board supported the government securities market during World War II and after, resulted in member banks becoming independent of Federal Reserve restraints.
   B. The United States Treasury must work through the Federal Reserve System to effect its purposes in relation to money and credit supply.
   C. Since the early 1920's, the Federal Reserve authorities have relied chiefly on open-market operations rather than rediscount rate changes as the method of credit control.
   D. The policy of gold sterilization in the 1930's kept gold coming into the country from increasing the excess reserves then prevailing in the banks.

7. Which of the following statements are CORRECT concerning the settlement of labor disputes in the United States?
   I. The Taft-Hartley Act prescribes conditions for reporting disputes to the Federal Mediation and Conciliation Service.
   II. Agents of the Federal Mediation and Conciliation Service may act as mediators or arbitrators, depending upon the circumstances of the case.
   III. If disputants agree to submit a dispute to arbitration by the Service, the decision is binding and refusal to abide by the award is punishable by criminal penalties.
   IV. The National Railroad Adjustment Board and the National Mediation Board handle railway labor disputes.
   V. The law establishing machinery for settling railway labor disputes forbids strikes on the railroads.

   The CORRECT answer is:

   A. I, II, IV
   B. I, IV
   C. II, III, V
   D. I, III, IV

8. Under the national emergency provisions of the Labor Management Relations Act of 1947 (Taft-Hartley),

   A. mediation of the dispute may be ordered by the President of the United States
   B. seizure of affected plants by the federal government is authorized if Congress concurs
   C. the federal government may obtain an injunction delaying a strike for eighty days
   D. compulsory arbitration may be invoked by the President

9. Which one of the following pairs is matched INCORRECTLY?

    A. Constant dollars - Price indexes
    B. Auto licenses - *Ability to pay* principle of taxation
    C. Net national product - Gross national product minus depreciation
    D. Secular stagnation - Keynes-Hansen thesis

10. The BASIC purpose of our federal and state conservation programs has been to

    A. preserve our natural resources for the purpose of ultimately deriving an important source of income for the federal budget
    B. aid the consumer by increasing the production of consumer goods and thus reducing prices
    C. help make our internal waterways, our forests, and our watersheds self-supporting and thus reduce the burden on government
    D. protect the public interest against treatment of our natural resources solely as sources of immediate income and not as capital assets

11. If the names Joseph A. Schumpeter, Wesley C. Mitchell, and A.F. Burns were mentioned in a discussion, the subject matter under discussion would be MOST likely that of

    A. money and banking
    B. business cycles
    C. housing
    D. social security

12. One of the MAJOR economic characteristics of the United States in the 1920's was a(n)

    A. low national income
    B. high degree of unemployment
    C. growing concentration of the control of industry
    D. increasing proportionate distribution of our national wealth among farmers, workers, and businessmen

13. Which one of the following aspects of the government's farm program has resulted in government ownership of large stocks of agricultural products?

    A. Nonrecourse loans
    B. *Soil bank* payments
    C. Export subsidies
    D. National School Lunch Program

14. An economist known for supporting the idea that some inflation is NOT necessarily an economic evil is

    A. Marcus Nadler
    B. G. Rowland Collins
    C. Paul A. Samuelson
    D. Sumner H. Slichter

15. Which one of the following is TRUE with regard to the consumer cooperative movement?

    A. The number of shares which one may buy is usually unlimited.
    B. Only members may purchase goods from the cooperative.
    C. All members of a consumer's cooperative have equal voting rights.
    D. An annual dividend based on profits is paid on each share.

16. Which one of the following was MOST unlike the other three in his social and political outlook?

    A. Robert Owen
    B. Mikhail Bakunin
    C. Louis Blanc
    D. Charles Fourier

17. The concept of the *economic man* in the history of economic thought relates to an individual who seeks to

    A. further his economic self-interest above anything else
    B. create a balance and equilibrium among the factors of consumption, production, distribution, and exchange
    C. make the superiority of capitalism over socialism a reality
    D. interpret politics mainly in the light of economic factors

18. According to the law of monopoly price, a monopolist will charge that price which will give him the

    A. greatest net profit
    B. highest price that consumers are willing to pay
    C. lowest cost of production
    D. greatest number of sales of his product

19. During the first decade of the 20th century, the American farmer enjoyed a period of comparatively sustained prosperity despite the fact that

    A. the number of his domestic competitors was increasing
    B. he was rapidly losing a large part of his foreign market
    C. his political influence was waning
    D. there was a deflationary movement after the discovery of gold in the Yukon

20. Unemployment which occurs when workers move from job to job is known as _____ unemployment.

    A. frictional
    B. seasonal
    C. technological
    D. cyclical

21. Which one of the following is INCORRECTLY matched?

    A. Joan Robinson - Imperfect Competition
    B. Edward H. Chamberlin - Monopolistic Competition
    C. Thorstein Veblen - Institutional Economics
    D. Francis A. Walker - Welfare Economics

22. According to the theories of J.M. Keynes, which one of the following factors is LEAST important in determining the level of employment and national income?

    A. Liquidity preference
    B. Wage bargaining between employers and employees
    C. The propensity to consume
    D. The marginal efficiency of capital

23. Which one of the following is NOT true concerning the various forms of business enterprise?

    A. Although approximately one-half of all manufacturing businesses in the United States are operated by single entrepreneurs, they account for only approximately ten percent of the manufactured output.
    B. Convertible bonds are those bonds which may be converted into income bonds on which interest is payable only if there are earnings by the corporation.
    C. Some securities are exempted from *blue-sky* laws because they are listed upon recognized stock exchanges.
    D. Some states have acted to help partnerships by laws permitting some limitation on the liability of the members.

24. Buying and selling the same commodity at the same time, but in two different markets, to take advantage of differences in the price of the commodity in the two places at the same instant, is known as

    A. hedging
    B. a joint operational cost
    C. arbitrage
    D. an open market operation

25. Which one of the following is NOT true concerning the control of credit by the federal government?
    The

    A. Securities and Exchange Commission can raise or lower margin requirements on stock sales
    B. Federal Reserve Board places certain restrictions on bank loans on real estate
    C. Federal Reserve Board may raise or lower the rediscount rate
    D. Federal Reserve Board does not control consumer credit at present

## KEY (CORRECT ANSWERS)

1. A
2. B
3. A
4. A
5. A

6. B
7. A
8. C
9. B
10. D

11. B
12. C
13. A
14. D
15. C

16. B
17. A
18. A
19. B
20. A

21. D
22. B
23. B
24. C
25. A

———

# TEST 2

DIRECTIONS: Each question or incomplete statement is followed by several suggested answers or completions. Select the one that BEST answers the question or completes the statement. *PRINT THE LETTER OF THE CORRECT ANSWER IN THE SPACE AT THE RIGHT.*

1. In the course of production of goods by the modern corporation, marginal costs are those costs which

    A. are considered variable costs
    B. are considered fixed costs
    C. result from a one-unit addition to output
    D. are obtained by dividing the total cost of production by the number of units produced

1._____

2. The OPTIMUM economic situation in regard to population in any country is

    A. that number of people whose labor will produce the largest possible per capita product
    B. the greatest number of people that country has ever had
    C. that time in a country's history of population where there has been developed the highest per capita income
    D. one in which there is a balance between industrial and agricultural workers

2._____

3. With which one of the following is the *iron law of wages* MOST closely associated?

    A. David Ricardo     B. Leon Walras
    C. Adam Smith        D. Alfred Marshall

3._____

4. A school of economic thought which had as its central doctrine the idea of the *net surplus* or the *product-net* was the

    A. physiocratic     B. classical
    C. institutional    D. mathematical

4._____

5. Which one of the following is a CORRECT statement in regard to the Federal Deposit Insurance Corporation?

    A. Insurance of bank deposits was included in the original Federal Reserve Act.
    B. The insurance maximum is currently $100,000 on each individual.
    C. The F.D.I.C. obtains its funds from government appropriations.
    D. All banks which have savings accounts are automatically eligible for F.D.I.C. protection.

5._____

6. Which one of the following statements concerning elasticity of demand in a system of private enterprise is TRUE?

    A. The demand for the product of each firm is elastic in a perfectly competitive industry.
    B. Demand becomes inelastic in a completely monopolistic situation.
    C. Elasticity of demand is increased when some firms in an industry obtain strong consumer preference.
    D. Elasticity of demand is increased in an imperfectly competitive industry.

6._____

7. Which one of the following is NOT a provision of the Taft-Hartley Law?

   A. Unions engaging in strikes or other activities which violate contracts with employers are subject to damage suits in the federal courts.
   B. Both prosecuting and judicial functions in administering the Taft-Hartley Law are combined in the NLRB.
   C. At least sixty days notice must be given by unions and employers before existing contracts may be modified or terminated.
   D. Featherbedding is included among labor practices prohibited by law.

8. Which one of the following is LEAST speculative in its operations? _____ transactions.

   A. Bear
   B. Bull
   C. Bucket shop
   D. Hedging

9. Which one of the following abuses in the public utility field did NOT lead to the passage of the Wheeler-Rayburn Act?

   A. Pyramided holding companies
   B. Issuance of watered stock
   C. *Milking* and *padding*
   D. Monopoly

10. A long term capital gain or loss occurs when the capital asset involved in the transaction is held

    A. six months or longer
    B. one year or longer
    C. eight months or longer
    D. eighteen months or longer

11. The term *dollar gap* is used in economic literature PRIMARILY in discussions of

    A. the federal budget
    B. international trade balances
    C. foreign exchange rates
    D. personal savings ratios

12. The doctrine of comparative costs is the underlying basis for the principle of

    A. protectionism
    B. mercantilism
    C. free trade
    D. colonialism

13. In which group do ALL of the items represent an enumeration of a corporation's working capital?

    A. Bank deposits, patent rights, franchises
    B. Finished products on hand, deposits in banks, accounts receivable
    C. Patent rights, franchises, raw materials on hand
    D. Deposits in banks, lands and buildings, machinery

14. Which one of the following is NOT a function of the Board of Governors of the Federal Reserve System?

    A. The determination of margin requirements for stock purchases
    B. The determination of the general monetary, credit, and operating policies of the Federal Reserve System
    C. The right to *review and determine* the rediscount rates
    D. The issuance of Federal Reserve notes

15. With which of the following areas of improvement was Frederick W. Taylor MOST concerned in his studies on scientific management?
    The

    A. handling of inventories, deliveries, and accounting practices
    B. improvement of welfare benefits through labor-management conferences
    C. performance of the individual worker at the individual's workplace
    D. performance of management

16. Which of the following governmental actions tend to aggravate inequality of income?
    I. Taxes on corporate profits
    II. Social Security payments
    III. Paying interest on the public debt
    IV. Sales taxes
    The CORRECT answer is:

    A. I, IV          B. III, IV          C. I, II          D. II, III

17. Which of the following forms of income is INCORRECTLY associated with its meaning?
    I. Disposable income - The total income earned by a worker
    II. Unearned income - Income received from returns on investments
    III. Real income - Amount of goods and services that can be bought for a dollar
    IV. Psychic income - Satisfaction derived by a doctor from owning a famous oil painting
    The CORRECT answer is:

    A. I, III          B. II *only*          C. II, IV          D. I *only*

18. Which one of the following was NOT a function of the United States Housing Authority?

    A. Insure against losses from mortgages held on real estate
    B. Grant aid for slum clearance
    C. Help in the building of low rent housing
    D. Grant loans to local public housing agencies

19. Which of the following functions did the Commodity Credit Corporation NOT exercise?

    A. Dispose of some surplus farm products through noncommercial channels
    B. Make loans on farm products to participating producers
    C. Buy some farm products to support their prices on the market
    D. Make direct payments to producers of perishable farm products sold at free market prices

20. Which one of the following statements about the TVA is NOT correct?

    A. Funds for expansion of its power plants are obtained from the sale of bonds.
    B. It uses its receipts from the sale of power to conduct its power business.
    C. Part of its activities is financed by annual appropriations of Congress.
    D. Atomic energy plants are among its largest customers.

21. Which of the following were provided for in the Wheeler-Lea Act of 1938?
    I. The FTC could act directly on its own initiative to suppress unfair business practices.
    II. It provided sufficient funds to permit the FTC to do an effective job in protecting consumers.
    III. It applied only to commodities sold in interstate trade or advertised across state lines.
    IV. The FTC could penalize advertisers only after appropriate court action had been successful.
    The CORRECT answer is:

    A. I, III          B. II, IV          C. I, II          D. III, IV

22. The purpose of the Miller-Tydings Act was to

    A. prevent the setting of monopoly prices by manufacturers
    B. prevent large chains from driving small retailers out of business
    C. prevent too great a spread between wholesale and retail prices
    D. encourage competition at the retail level

23. Which of the following are characteristic of a consumer cooperative that has adopted the Rochdale form of organization?
    I. If a profit is made, consumer-members may receive patronage dividends.
    II. Consumer-members may purchase their necessities both on a cash and credit basis.
    III. In order to ensure a democratic control, each member in the cooperative is given a maximum of one vote.
    IV. The rate of interest on shares varies with cooperative earnings.
    The CORRECT answer is:

    A. I, III          B. I, II          C. II, IV          D. III, IV

24. Which of the following pairs presents a significant contrast in terms of labor gains in the United States?

    A. Commonwealth v. Hunt, 1842 - National Labor Relations Act, 1935
    B. Clayton Act, 1914 - Adamson Act, 1916
    C. Danbury Hatters Case, 1908 - National Recovery Act, 1933
    D. Seamen's Act, 1916 - Fair Labor Standards Act, 1938

25. Which of the following provisions is NOT contained in the Taft-Hartley Act?

    A. Providing for a reconstruction of the NLRB
    B. Broadening the legal rights of employers
    C. Increasing the responsibility of labor unions
    D. Outlawing the union shop and maintenance of membership classes

## KEY (CORRECT ANSWERS)

1. C
2. A
3. A
4. A
5. B

6. A
7. B
8. D
9. D
10. B

11. B
12. C
13. B
14. D
15. C

16. B
17. D
18. A
19. D
20. A

21. A
22. B
23. A
24. C
25. D

# TEST 3

DIRECTIONS: Each question or incomplete statement is followed by several suggested answers or completions. Select the one that BEST answers the question or completes the statement. *PRINT THE LETTER OF THE CORRECT ANSWER IN THE SPACE AT THE RIGHT.*

1. Which of the following statements are CORRECT as regards the Malthusian theory?  1.____
    I. As population increases, food supply will increase proportionally.
    II. Population increases in geometric ratio, while food supply increases in arithmetic ratio.
    III. Population, unless curbed by natural and other forces, tends to outrun food supply.
    IV. Conditions in highly industrialized countries have challenged the general applicability of the Malthusian theory.
   The CORRECT answer is:

   A. I, II  
   B. II, III, IV  
   C. I, II, IV  
   D. III, IV, I

2. Which of the following statements are attributable to Karl Marx?  2.____
    I. A preceding generation cannot bind a succeeding one by its laws or controls.
    II. The history of all hitherto existing societies is the history of class struggle.
    III. This country with its institutions belongs to the people who inhabit it.
    IV. Workingmen of all countries unite.
   The CORRECT answer is:

   A. I, II  B. II, IV  C. I, III  D. III, I

3. Which statement does NOT correctly characterize the reasons for the deep and prevailing dissatisfaction of institutional economists with neo-classical economic doctrines?  3.____

   A. Marshallian economics does not come to grips with present-day problems.
   B. Neo-classicism is but a refurbishing of generalizations made a century and more ago by the classicists in defense of the then ruling English classes.
   C. Institutionalists emphasize individual behavior along with value and price.
   D. Institutionalists' chief interest is in man-made institutions.

4. Which of the following statements regarding the *single tax* theory of Henry George are TRUE?  4.____
    I. It rests on the assumption that individual human labor constitutes the only justifiable title to property.
    II. His social philosophy is based on the fundamental distinction between land and capital.
    III. The application would be difficult since it necessitates separating the value of the land from the value of its improvements.
    IV. The modern single tax movement has done much to pave the way for a more equitable distribution of taxation.
   The CORRECT answer is:

   A. I, II, III, IV  
   B. I, III  
   C. I, II, IV  
   D. III, IV

5. Which one of these ideas was NOT expressed by Adam Smith in THE WEALTH OF NATIONS?

   A. The recurrence of business cycles
   B. The principle of free trade
   C. The principle of free competition
   D. A nation's wealth consists of more than gold and silver

6. Which one of the following economists can be LEAST properly grouped with the other three?

   A. William Stanley Jevons
   B. Leon Walras
   C. Francois Quesnay
   D. Vilfredo Pareto

7. Which one of the following economists advanced the theory that an increase in wages to workers would result in improved standards which would, in turn, beget larger families, increase the labor supply, and, thus, force wages down?

   A. David Ricardo
   B. Charles Fourier
   C. Robert Owen
   D. Frederick Bastiat

8. Which one of the following is NOT one of the advantages of a corporation as a form of business organization?

   A. It insures a continuity of existence regardless of the life span of individuals.
   B. It makes possible the amassing of large amounts of capital in one business.
   C. Stockholders are relieved of all liability for losses in case of business failure.
   D. It affords the business certain privileges and immunities of a person before the law.

9. Which of the following was NOT a reason for the passage of the Gold Standard Act of 1900?

   A. Fresh gold deposits had been recently discovered in Alaska, Australia, and South Africa, assuring an adequate supply for the backing of paper currency
   B. The quantity of paper currency in circulation was shrinking because the public refused to buy bonds to finance the Spanish-American War.
   C. The victory of the Republican Party in the election was viewed as a rejection of bimetallism.
   D. The farmer was enjoying a temporary prosperity brought on by foreign crop failures.

10. Which of the following is an INCORRECT application of the *safety valve* theory of agriculture and the frontier as it affected labor?

    A. There is little evidence that the existence of cheap lands operated in any effective fashion to raise wages of industrial labor.
    B. Throughout the period of industrialism, the movement of population from the country to the city had been greater than the movement from the city to the country.
    C. The frontier did attract millions of immigrants and discontented townsmen from East and South who might have been forced into the ranks of industrial labor.
    D. The *new* immigrants from Eastern and Southern Europe, by settling in large numbers in the West, had little influence on industrial labor.

11. Which of the following BEST illustrates the United States' withdrawal from economic isolation?
    The

    A. Johnson Debt Default Act of 1934
    B. Hawley-Smoot Tariff Act of 1930
    C. Reciprocal Trade Agreements Act of 1934
    D. Neutrality Acts of 1935-37

12. The function of the International Monetary Fund is to

    A. provide loans to backward nations for industrial development
    B. stabilize national currencies
    C. make loans for foreign trade
    D. serve as a clearing house for reparation

13. Which one of the following statements BEST describes the relation of the NRA of 1933 to the Sherman Act of 1890 and the Clayton Act of 1914?
    The NRA

    A. was the first to provide penalties for the creation of combinations in restraint of trade
    B. restated the *open shop* principles first formulated in the Sherman Act
    C. suspended the earlier anti-trust laws
    D. applied anti-trust measures to public utilities which were exempt under the earlier acts

14. Which of the following is a function of the Securities Exchange Commission?
    It

    A. sets margin requirements
    B. regulates prices on commodity exchanges
    C. registers securities sold in interstate commerce
    D. sets maximum rates charged by public utilities other than railroads

15. In which of the following pairs does the SECOND item represent a halt or reversal in legislation direction of the FIRST?

    A. Interstate Commerce Act - Hepburn Act
    B. Sherman Act - Clayton Act
    C. Norris-LaGuardia Act - Taft-Hartley Act
    D. Pure Food and Drugs Act - Wheeler-Lea Act

16. The statistical measure that shows the production of the country in terms of expenditures for goods and services is the

    A. index of commodity prices            B. index of business activity
    C. cost-of-living index                 D. gross national product

17. President Clinton's stated policy concerning the government's farm program revealed opposition to _____ price supports.

    A. reciprocal                           B. rigid
    C. any type of                          D. flexible

18. The CHIEF reason as to why indirect taxes do not meet the principles of good taxation is that they

   A. cost too much to collect
   B. are too easy to evade
   C. are too annoying for the taxpayer
   D. are regressive

19. To determine the yield he will receive from a government bond, the investor should consider the _____ the bond.

   A. interest rate on
   B. face value and interest rate of
   C. price he pays for it and interest rate of
   D. maturity date and interest rate of

20. Which of the following are ESSENTIAL characteristics of a gold standard?
   I. The money unit is a definite weight and fineness of gold.
   II. There is convertibility of all other forms of money into gold.
   III. There is free and unlimited coinage of gold.
   IV. There is a restricted gold market with other countries.
   V. Gold is legal tender.

   The CORRECT answer is:

   A. I, II, III, IV
   B. I, II, III, V
   C. II, III, IV, V
   D. I, IV, V

21. The MOST significant difference between demand deposits and time deposits in business practice today is that

   A. advance notice is required before demand deposits may be withdrawn
   B. separate banks must be used to maintain each of the two kinds of deposits
   C. demand deposits do not earn interest
   D. only time deposits may be insured by the F.D.C.

22. Basic to the understanding of our modern industrial society is the concept that saving and investment are

   A. generally done by different people for different reasons
   B. synonymous terms
   C. generally done by the same people for a variety of reasons
   D. always equal

23. Which of the following statements regarding commercial banks are TRUE?
   I. Their loans create deposits.
   II. Most of their loans are for short terms.
   III. Their loans are primarily for the purpose of furthering profitable business enterprises.
   IV. They do not pay interest on commercial deposits.

   The CORRECT answer is:

   A. I, II
   B. III, IV
   C. I, II, IV
   D. I, II, III, IV

24. The power to fix margin requirements for trading in stocks is based upon authority granted in the

    A. Securities Exchange Act
    B. Federal Trade Commission Act
    C. Federal Reserve Act
    D. Federal Deposit Insurance Corporation Law

25. Which one of the following statements concerning the Norris-LaGuardia Act and its provisions is NOT true?

    A. It was passed during the Hoover Administration.
    B. Contracts under which employees agreed not to join free unions were enforceable only in federal courts.
    C. An injunction could be issued only after a hearing in open court with both parties present.
    D. Labor's right to organize should be protected by the United States government.

## KEY (CORRECT ANSWERS)

| | | | |
|---|---|---|---|
| 1. B | | 11. C | |
| 2. B | | 12. B | |
| 3. C | | 13. C | |
| 4. A | | 14. C | |
| 5. A | | 15. C | |
| 6. C | | 16. D | |
| 7. A | | 17. B | |
| 8. C | | 18. D | |
| 9. B | | 19. C | |
| 10. D | | 20. B | |

21. C
22. A
23. D
24. A
25. B

# TEST 4

DIRECTIONS: Each question or incomplete statement is followed by several suggested answers or completions. Select the one that BEST answers the question or completes the statement. *PRINT THE LETTER OF THE CORRECT ANSWER IN THE SPACE AT THE RIGHT.*

1. Which one of the following is NOT an aspect of our federal social security system?

    A. Retirement payments to wives of insured workers collecting benefits
    B. Payments to insured workers temporarily not working because of disability
    C. Payments for surviving dependent children of insured workers
    D. Lump-sum payments on death of insured workers.

1._____

2. Which of the following statements regarding the Taft-Hartley Act are TRUE?
    I. All newly hired workers must join a union within a given period of time.
    II. Secondary boycotts are outlawed.
    III. A union may be sued for damages if it violates a contract.
    IV. Jurisdictional disputes are illegal.
    V. Employers may apply for injunctions to prevent a strike where the national welfare is involved.

    The CORRECT answer is:

    A. I, II, III, IV, V  B. II, III, IV
    C. III, IV, I, II     D. III, IV, II, V

2._____

3. As a result of the Employment Act of 1946, there is at present a

    A. standby program of public works
    B. federal unemployment insurance program
    C. federal employment service
    D. council of economic advisers

3._____

4. According to Gresham's Law, under bimetallism, the metal which will be driven out of circulation is

    A. more expensive per ounce in the open market
    B. more expensive per ounce in the mint
    C. valued at a lower ratio by the mint than in the market
    D. valued at a higher ratio by the mint than in the market

4._____

5. Which of the following would be APPROPRIATE illustrations of the basic principles of capital formation?
    I. A steel worker signs up for payroll deductions under his company's stock purchase plan
    II. A farmer buys a tractor instead of a sedan
    III. A corporation *passes a dividend* at the end of a profitable year
    IV. A bank's use of savings deposits to purchase railroad bonds

    The CORRECT answer is:

    A. I, III, IV    B. I, II, IV
    C. II, III, IV   D. I, II, III, IV

5._____

6. Which of the following dynamic forces or trends would exert a depressing or elevating effect on normal price?
   I. Increase of population
   II. Monetary disturbances
   III. Increase in - real wages
   IV. Rise in the per unit expense of marketing
   The CORRECT answer is:

   A. I, II, III
   B. I, II, III, IV
   C. III, IV, I
   D. II, III, IV

7. Economists today GENERALLY agree that the equilibrium level of national income _____ the level of full employment of resources.

   A. may be above
   B. may be below
   C. must be above
   D. must be below

8. Which does NOT help to create a favorable balance of trade for a nation?

   A. *Blocked currency*
   B. Devaluation of currency
   C. Export licensing
   D. Payment of dividends by foreign firms

9. Though they are industrial giants, none of the Big Three automobile companies makes its own paint and finishes and only one makes its own steel.
   This illustration is MOST directly pertinent to a discussion of

   A. factors affecting industrial concentration
   B. basing point pricing and monopoly
   C. geographic division of labor
   D. disadvantages of the corporation

10. Which one of the following would be LEAST satisfactory as an explanation of a period of decline in the business cycle?

    A. Profitability of introduction of new capital goods starts to fall
    B. Planned savings fail to equal planned investment
    C. Volume of saving increases in relation to rate of consumption
    D. Tendency for costs to rise in a period of expansion

11. In teaching the problem of causes of inflation, emphasis should be placed on the relationship between

    A. purchasing power and demand for goods
    B. quantity of money and demand for goods
    C. purchasing power and supply of goods
    D. quantity of money and price level

12. A teacher uses this illustration: 30 minutes of a United States textile machine operator's time are needed to buy a pound of coffee.
    The class is PROBABLY discussing

    A. price fixing
    B. variable costs
    C. international trade
    D. diminishing returns

13. Which one of the following economists does NOT belong in the same classification with the other three?

    A. Alfred Marshall
    B. Wesley C. Mitchell
    C. John R. Commons
    D. Thorstein Veblen

14. With which of the following is Thorstein Veblen LEAST properly associated?

    A. The Institutional School
    B. *The Theory of the Leisure Class*
    C. The defense of *the economic man*
    D. The concept of *conspicuous consumption*

15. Which one of the following does NOT belong in a list of *scientific socialists*?

    A. Karl Marx
    B. Robert Owen
    C. Friedrich Engels
    D. Carl Rodbertus

16. Which of the following economists is NOT generally associated with the *wages fund theory*?

    A. Nassau William Senior
    B. Thomas Malthus
    C. William S. Jevons
    D. James Mill

17. Which one of the following books deals PRIMARILY with the problem of secular trends rather than short-term fluctuations in national income?

    A. Burns & Mitchell - MEASURING BUSINESS CYCLES
    B. Von Haberler - PROSPERITY AND DEPRESSION
    C. Estey - BUSINESS CYCLE THEORY
    D. Hansen - FULL RECOVERY OR STAGNATION

18. Buying and selling at the same time, the one transaction being in the actual present market and the other in the future speculative market, is called

    A. selling short
    B. manipulation
    C. arbitrage
    D. hedging

19. The MAIN contention in favor of Henry George's SINGLE TAX is that

    A. economic rent is a social product
    B. it is based on ability to pay
    C. its cost of collection is low
    D. it directs use of land into socially beneficial fields

20. The objection of business to the demands of labor for a guaranteed annual wage are based on the facts that
    I. the labor force would tend to lose mobility
    II. new industries would have difficulty in finding employees
    III. labor turnover would increase
    IV. it would be more difficult to make price cuts to meet competition
    The CORRECT answer is:

    A. I, III
    B. I, II, III, IV
    C. II, IV
    D. I, II, IV

21. Comparing the percentage rise in the general price level during World War I with that during World War II, it is MOST accurate to state that

    A. there was little difference in the percentage rise
    B. prices rose more rapidly during World War II
    C. prices rose more rapidly during World War I
    D. there is no method of making a statistical evaluation

22. The emphasis of the New Deal on *pump priming* indicated reliance on the monetary philosophy of

    A. Alfred Marshall
    B. Wesley C. Mitchell
    C. J.M. Keynes
    D. Simon Kuznets

23. Which of the following situations are the effects of a large volume of public debt?
    I. Increased dependency of nation's banks on Treasury policy
    II. Increased inflationary pressures
    III. Increased efficiency of the tax structure
    IV. Expansion of the tax system into new areas

    The CORRECT answer is:

    A. I, II, IV
    B. I, II, III, IV
    C. I, II
    D. III, IV

24. The economic factors which may determine the quantity of money and credit in circulation are
    I. the form in which the public wishes to hold its liquid assets
    II. deficit financing by the United States government
    III. an increase in loans by commercial banks
    IV. importation of gold

    The CORRECT answer is:

    A. I, III, IV
    B. III, IV
    C. I, II
    D. I, II, III, IV

25. Which of the following may back Federal Reserve notes?
    I. Gold certificates
    II. Commercial paper
    III. Government securities
    IV. Treasury notes of 1890

    The CORRECT answer is:

    A. I, II, III
    B. II, III, IV
    C. II, IV
    D. I, III

## KEY (CORRECT ANSWER)

1. B
2. B
3. D
4. C
5. D

6. B
7. B
8. C
9. A
10. B

11. C
12. C
13. A
14. C
15. B

16. C
17. D
18. D
19. A
20. D

21. C
22. C
23. A
24. D
25. A

# TEST 5

DIRECTIONS: Each question or incomplete statement is followed by several suggested answers or completions. Select the one that BEST answers the question or completes the statement. *PRINT THE LETTER OF THE CORRECT ANSWER IN THE SPACE AT THE RIGHT.*

1. The MAIN controls of the Federal Reserve System over the supply of money and credit are weakened when

   A. excess reserves of member banks increase
   B. the President suspends their use by Executive Order
   C. the Federal Reserve System raises the rediscount rate
   D. the Federal Reserve Bank conducts an open market operation

2. The establishment of which of the following resulted from an agreement arrived at by the international conference at Bretton Woods in 1944?
   I. International Monetary Fund
   II. International Bank for Reconstruction and Development
   III. International Trade Organization
   IV. European Recovery Plan

   The CORRECT answer is:

   A. I, II, III           B. I, II
   C. II, III              D. I, III, IV

3. Thorstein Veblen's theory that the modern economic system creates two types of values, economic and pecuniary, resulted in his conclusion that there is a basic difference between

   A. capital and labor
   B. industry and business
   C. government and the consumer
   D. trade and industrial unions

4. Which of the following statements CORRECTLY characterize American agriculture during the decade 1923-1932?
   I. Federal legislation was passed with a view to stabilizing the supply of farm products.
   II. With 1909-1914 as a base, farm prices were above parity during the first half and fell below parity during the second half of the period.
   III. The proportion of agricultural supplement to total employment declined.
   IV. The number of farms remained fairly constant.

   The CORRECT answer is:

   A. I, II, IV           B. I, II, III
   C. II, III, IV         D. I, III, IV

5. The situation in which a worker need NOT be a union member to be hired but must become and remain a union member to continue to be employed is known as a

   A. union shop          B. closed shop
   C. open shop           D. open union

6. Berle and Means, in THE MODERN CORPORATION AND PRIVATE PROPERTY, conclude that corporate control lies in the hands of

    A. the majority of stockholders
    B. investment banks
    C. those who have actual power to select the Board of Directors
    D. the largest investors in the corporation

7. Farm cooperatives are exempt from the provisions of the anti-trust laws as a result of the _____ Act.

    A. Webb-Pomerene
    B. Capper-Volstead
    C. Robinson-Patman
    D. Anderson

8. The American economist MOST closely associated with the study of business cycles is

    A. John R. Commons
    B. Wesley C. Mitchell
    C. Selig Perlman
    D. John Bates Clark

9. Which one of the following may CORRECTLY be considered the result of the other three?

    A. Legislation in the state of Wisconsin
    B. Social Security Act
    C. Townsend Plan
    D. Report of the Brookings Institution

10. Of the following items, the one with the LOWEST degree of elastic demand is

    A. sirloin steak
    B. beef
    C. food
    D. meat

11. The Randall Commission recommended

    A. higher protective tariffs
    B. a Buy-American program
    C. the extension of reciprocal tariffs
    D. the removal of tariffs

12. All of the following factors may account for the strengthening of the British pound EXCEPT

    A. decreased imports of gold
    B. increased British exports
    C. decreased imports from the dollar area
    D. lifting of wartime restrictions on exchange rates

13. A function of the International Monetary Fund is to

    A. grant loans of a self-liquidating nature to underdeveloped countries
    B. provide stability in foreign exchange rates while allowing freedom of action in coping with domestic problems
    C. grant loans for relief and rehabilitation to members of the United Nations who sustained extensive damage during World War II
    D. prevent the flight of capital from countries with unstable currencies

14. A number of chain stores receiving rebates from manufacturers have been prosecuted in violation of the _____ Act.

   A. Miller-Tydings
   B. Wheeler-Rayburn
   C. Copeland-Lea
   D. Robinson-Patman

15. A 6% sales tax on EVERY purchase of ANY kind would be, in effect,

   A. proportional
   B. inelastic
   C. progressive
   D. regressive

16. Which one of the following is NOT a device for achieving minority control of corporations?

   A. The holding company
   B. Non-voting stock
   C. The voting trust
   D. The joint-stock company

17. Which of the following ACCURATELY contrasts a corporation and a consumers' cooperative?

   A. One vote per share; one vote per member
   B. Chartered by the state; no charter of incorporation
   C. Profits paid out as dividends; profits eliminated by charging low prices
   D. Issue stock; no stock issued

18. The capital of a corporation is represented by $400,000 of 5% bonds and $200,000 of common stock. The corporation goes into bankruptcy, and its assets yield $100,000. The amount so realized is distributed as follows:
   _____ to bondholders, _____ to stockholders.

   A. $80,000; $20,000
   B. nothing; $100,000
   C. $50,000; $50,000
   D. $100,000; nothing

19. In the following paired items, the pair that contains examples of items from the two sides of a balance sheet is

   A. inventory and good will
   B. accounts receivable and surplus
   C. notes payable and capital stock
   D. cash and operating expenses

20. The International Ladies Garment Workers Union is a(n)
   I. industrial union
   II. vertical union
   III. affiliated with the C.I.O.
   IV. independent union
   The CORRECT answer is:

   A. I, II
   B. I, II, III
   C. I, III, IV
   D. II, III

21. Each of the following agencies has authority to fix some price or rate EXCEPT the 21.____

   A. Board of Governors of the Federal Reserve System
   B. SEC
   C. ICC
   D. Public Service Commission

22. In the matter of appraising the value of public utilities for purposes of rate regulation, the Supreme Court has 22.____

   A. adopted the theory of prudent cost less depreciation
   B. favored the theory of reproduction cost
   C. given no clear-cut support to either doctrine
   D. ruled that each state may set up its own guides for its public service commissions

23. The risks due to speculative production tend to be increased by 23.____

   A. improved transportation
   B. improved market information
   C. monopoly
   D. the roundabout method of production

24. The equation $\dfrac{MV + M'V'}{T} = P$ 24.____

   A. was formulated to explain why wages lag behind prices
   B. is related to the quantity theory of money
   C. obviates the need for index numbers in measuring price changes
   D. was evolved by Adam Smith

25. Indicate by reference to the groupings below which of the following statements are TRUE about wages. 25.____
   I. Wages are determined in accordance with the same general principles which apply to all prices.
   II. An increase in the supply of capital tends to raise wages.
   III. The current level of wages is a determinant of the demand for labor.
   IV. Wage differentials result from the existence of non-competing groups.
   
   The CORRECT answer is:

   A. I, III
   B. II, IV
   C. I, III, IV
   D. I, II, II, IV

## KEY (CORRECT ANSWERS)

1. A
2. B
3. B
4. D
5. A

6. C
7. B
8. B
9. B
10. C

11. C
12. A
13. B
14. D
15. D

16. D
17. A
18. D
19. B
20. A

21. B
22. C
23. D
24. B
25. D

# A SURVEY OF THE IDEAS OF THE GREAT ECONOMISTS

## ADAM SMITH (1723-1790)

In the Wealth of Nations, first published in 1776, Adam Smith was concerned with an analysis of two broad problems: the market mechanism which holds society together, and the dynamic movement of society over time.

1. MARKET MECHANISM: Smith's laws of the free market demonstrate how the interaction of self-interest among individuals results in competition, which in turn provides society with those goods and services it wants, at the prices society is willing to pay, and in the quantities society desires. This comes about in the following manner:

(a) Self-Interest: Adam Smith assumed that all individuals are motivated by self-interest. The desire to get ahead and advance economically is part of the make-up of all persons, causing them to work in whatever capacity society is willing to pay for. Smith asserted that "it is not from the benevolence of the butcher, the brewer, or the baker, that we expect our dinner, but from regard to their own self-interest. We address ourselves not to their humanity, but to their self-love, and never talk to them of our necessities but of their advantages."

(b) Competition: Self-interest is regulated by competition, the logical outcome of the free play of conflicting self-interests. Each person trying to maximize his own gain is in competition with similarly motivated individuals, which prevents each one's self-interest from getting out of hand. If a shopkeeper charges too much for his goods, in the hope of making excessive profits, he will lose business to his competitors, who will undersell him. If he refuses to pay acceptable wages, his employees will find work elsewhere, at higher wages, and he will be left without workers. Collusive agreements to fix prices will be broken by an independent producer, selling below the monopolistic price. The laws of the market not only insure a competitive price, but also see to it that the goods produced are in the quantities desired by society. If there is a surplus of radios and a shortage of television sets, the price of the former will fall and the price of the latter will rise. Workers will be released from the radio industry, cutting down the output of the radios, as a result of the decline in profits. These temporarily unemployed workers will be absorbed by the increased demand for labor in the television industry. The ultimate result of these shifts will be exactly what society wants: an increase in television production and a decrease in radio production. The interaction of supply and demand in the free market also regulates the incomes of the productive factors. If the wages of steel workers are out of line with wages in comparable occupations, there will be a shift of workers to the steel industry, causing wages there to fall. In conclusion, *Adam Smith's laws of the market, assuming self-interest and competition exist, provide society with a self-regulating mechanism.*

2. DYNAMIC MOVEMENT OF SOCIETY: The wealth and standard of living of society increase over the years. This is partly the result of the market mechanism, which propels men to work, to innovate, and to take risks. Smith believed that the increase in productivity of society was the result of two additional factors. First, capital

accumulation, generated by the profits of the system, led to more machinery and equipment, expanding the division of labor and leading to greater riches. This increased the demand for labor, which increased wages and reduced the source of accumulation (profits). The second factor, the growth of population in response to the increased demand for workers, reduced wages, restored profits, and led to further capital accumulation.

3. CONCLUSION: The workings of the market mechanism, which beneficially harnesses the self-interests of individuals, and the natural trend of the nation's standard of living led Adam Smith to favor a governmental policy of *laissez-faire*. Smith was against the government meddling with the free market mechanism. He was protesting against the many government economic regulations in 18th century England.

## DAVID RICARDO (1772-1823)

Ricardo amassed a fortune early in life as a stockbroker, which enabled him to retire from business at an early age and to devote himself to intellectual pursuits. The Principles of Political Economy and Taxation, published first in 1817, is his most important work. In this book Ricardo was interested primarily in the theory of value and distribution. Ricardo's theory is best understood by dividing it into three sections: the theory of value; the theory of wages, profit and rent; and the theory of economic development.

1. THE THEORY OF VALUE: The relative value of commodities (i.e. exchange value) is determined according to Ricardo from scarcity of labor. Great art works are valued not by the quantity of labor bestowed upon them, but by their scarcity. However, most commodities in a capitalist system are capable of infinite reproduction. The comparable value of these commodities is determined by the quantity of labor contained in them. Thus, if good X contains four hours of labor and good Y contains two hours of labor, good X will be worth twice as much as good Y. In advanced economies, Ricardo argued that not only present but also past labor, embodied in machinery, tools, buildings, etc., determine the relative value of commodities. In this case, the worker's remuneration is less than the value of the commodity, the difference being the capitalist's profit.

2. THE THEORY OF WAGES, PROFIT AND RENT: Ricardo distinguished between two types of wages: the natural price of labor and the market price of labor. The former is that which is "necessary to enable the laborers, one with another, to subsist and to perpetuate their race, without either increase or diminution." The latter is determined by the current market conditions in accordance with supply and demand; but it will gravitate towards the natural price. If wages are above the subsistence level (i.e., the natural price), population will increase, primarily, as a result of a decline in the mortality rate of infants and young children, and the wages of labor will fall. Ricardo's theory of wages is often called the *iron law of wages*.

The return to capital, which Ricardo called the profit rate, is set by the interaction of supply and demand. In this connection, Ricardo pointed out that competition among capitalists tends to establish a uniform profit rate. For example, when the profit rate of an industry is relatively high, capital will be attracted into the industry, bringing down the profit rate.

Ricardo believed that rent is derived from differences in the fertility of soil. The market price of an agricultural product must be sufficient to cover its cost of production on the poorest soil. Thus, on the least fertile land the cost of production will equal the price of the product. However, a surplus or profit will appear on better quality land since the cost of production will be less than the market price. This surplus will be extracted by the landowner from the tenant farmer due to competition among tenants for better land. Ricardo argued that in the course of time poorer quality lands would be cultivated in order to feed the rising population, resulting in larger surpluses which would increase the rentier's share of national income relative to the labor and capitalist class. This conclusion of Ricardo's *differential theory of rent* provided the rising industrialist class with a powerful weapon against the landed interests.

3. THE THEORY OF ECONOMIC DEVELOPMENT: In the future, progressively poorer lands will be cultivated, leading to higher food prices. This in turn will force upward money wages to enable the working class to maintain its subsistence level. Since Ricardo alleged that profits and wages are inversely related, capital accumulation, which directly depends upon profits, will fall and hence future economic progress will be restricted. Ricardo's analysis of economic development means that the interest of the landlord is opposed to the general welfare of society, as well as the interest of the capitalist and labor classes. The theory of differential rent is at the heart of Ricardo's pessimistic interpretation of the natural course of economic progress. However, Ricardo overlooked the fact that improved technology would offset the increasing use of less fertile lands, causing future food prices to fall.

## THOMAS MALTHUS (1772-1834)

Malthus's most significant contribution to economic thought is contained in his <u>Essay on the Principle of Population</u>, published first in 1798. In this work Malthus alleged that population tended to increase in a geometrical progression (1, 2, 4, 8, 16, 32...) while the subsistence level of food output tended to increase in an arithmetical progression (1, 2, 3, 4, 5, 6...). The tendency for population to outrun the food supply would be checked by two methods: positive and preventive. Positive checks such as famines, diseases and wars increased the death rate. Preventive checks, on the other hand, such as moral restraint, diminished the birth rate. Malthus, who was a parson, naturally advocated moral restraint, by which he meant abstention from marriage until one was financially able to support a family. Malthus was against poor relief because it aggravated the problem by encouraging the poor to have children.

1. BASIS FOR POPULATION THEORY: Both Malthus' theory of population and Ricardo's theory of differential rent are based on the famous law of diminishing returns. The increase in differential rent over time, postulated by Ricardo, arises because the cultivation of inferior land means that the cost of a unit of agricultural output increases as output is expanded (i.e. diminishing returns), making it progressively more difficult to provide subsistence for a growing population. Malthus and Ricardo both underestimated the powerful effects the opening up of new areas and the improvement in technology would have on the world's food supply.

## JOHN STUART MILL (1806-1873)

In 1848 Mill published his <u>Principles of Political Economy</u>, which surveyed the whole field of economics, retracing and updating many of the principles on rent, wages, profits, prices and taxes previously analyzed by Smith, Ricardo and Malthus. However, Mill made a very important contribution of his own by pointing out the applicability of economic laws to production and to distribution.

1. PRODUCTION: Economic laws only apply to production. These impersonal laws are not arbitrary but are closely related to limits nature imposes on productivity (i.e. diminishing returns in agriculture). They tell us how to maximize output given the relative scarcity of resources.

2. DISTRIBUTION: The distribution of output is unrelated to the laws of economics. Mill argued that "the laws and conditions of the production of wealth partake of the character of physical truths. There is nothing optional or arbitrary in them ... It is not so with the Distribution of Wealth. That is a matter of human institution solely. The things once there, mankind, individually or collectively, can do with them as they like ... The Distribution of Wealth, therefore, depends on the laws and customs of society." This conclusion permitted Mill to favor laissez-faire in the sphere of production, and at the same time advocate reforms aimed at redistributing income in favor of the poor. Even if the natural course of real wages is downward, society could alter this natural result by taxing income and subsidizing the low-income families. Mill argued that there are no economic forces to justify the sharing of society's wealth. Thus, Mill's recognition that distribution was determined solely by human action allowed him to view the world optimistically, hoping that mankind, guided by reason, would progress and improve social welfare.

## KARL MARX (1816 -1883)

Marx was a revolutionist who used the study of economics as a theoretical mechanism to condemn a social system which he despised. Two great forces influenced Marx's thinking. The first was the new industrial society of the 19th century, and the second was the philosophy of Hegel. From Hegel's dialectic principle, Marx drew his notion of contradiction as the cause of social change.

1. DIALECTIC MATERIALISM: Society sets up a particular economic structure (i.e. the ownership of the means of production) to enable society to utilize to the fullest its productive powers. However, the continual increase in productive power brings society into a conflict with the economic structure it has created. The economic structure and the productive power are out of line. The former has not kept pace with the latter, and as a result the economic structure of society is inappropriate for its productive powers. To illustrate, the earliest economic structure was characterized by common ownership of the means of production, which at that time was merely land. As productive powers improved, society was able to produce a surplus above the subsistence level. This surplus was appropriated by individuals, making private property an integral part of the economic structure. The first form of private property, Marx argued, was the ancient slave states in which private ownership included man himself. When slave states became inadequate, they gave way to feudalism, and this in turn was replaced by capitalism. To the latter Marx also applies the concept of dialectic materialism and,

therefore, he viewed capitalism and its system of private property in historical perspective as being a temporary phase of economic development. The inherent contradiction in capitalism, forcing it to give way to another economic structure, is the conflict between the interests of the proletariat and the interests of the capitalists. The struggle between capital and labor is the inevitable outcome of the economic structure, where the former owns the means of production and the latter owns nothing but labor power.

2. THE LABOR THEORY OF VALUE: Workers sell their labor to capitalists for exactly what it is worth (its value). This saleable value is the wage the worker needs in order to subsist. In other words, the value of labor is equivalent to a wage that will keep the laborer alive. If the wage of labor is $.50 per hour and four hours work per day is necessary for the worker to subsist, the value of labor or its worth is $2.00 a day. However, the worker does not contract to work merely four hours each day, but agrees to work a ten- or twelve-hour day. Thus, profits accrue to the capitalist because he obtains the produce of twelve hours worth of value, which he sells in the market, at a cost of four. Marx terms the portion of unpaid work surplus value. The worker gets paid his true value, but at the same time he is cheated for he must work longer than the hours required to subsist. This situation arises because the capitalist, by owning the means of production, can refuse a worker a job (i.e. his means of subsistence) unless he agrees to work a full day.

3. COMPETITION AMONG THE CAPITALISTS: Motivated by the desire to accumulate, capitalists are always trying to increase the scale of their operations. This leads to an increased demand for the services of labor, which bids up their wages and hence lowers surplus value. Smith and Ricardo also argued that profits would be narrowed by rising wages. However, they alleged that profits would be restored by the tendency of the working class to increase their numbers with every increase in wages. Marx could not accept the Malthusian answer to the profit problem because it viewed the proletariat, the future rulers of society, as being shortsighted and ignorant. For Marx, the capitalist meets the dilemma of rising wages by introducing labor-saving machinery into his factory. As a consequence, workers thrown out of jobs form an "Industrial Reserve Army," which leads to greater competition for jobs, lowering wages to their former subsistence level. The introduction of labor-saving machinery means that the capitalist is substituting non-profitable means of production for profitable ones which ultimately must lead to a reduction in profits. Unemployment appears again as capitalists continue their drive for accumulation. These crises worsen with the introduction of more non-profitable means of production, and eventually the system is overthrown by the workers.

4. THE FUTURE: The successor to capitalism would be a classless state where private property would be eliminated and the means of production would be owned by society. A proletariat dictatorship would be set up during a transitional period which would evolve into pure communism.

## ALFRED MARSHALL (1842-1924)

Marshall was determined that economics should continue as a productive science which would guide statesmen and influence policy. His theoretical analysis was aimed at maintaining this contact between economic theory and policy. Marshall's major work is his Principles of Economics, published originally in 1890. Some of Marshall's more important contributions are provided below.

1. VALUE: Marshall argued that the forces behind supply and demand determine value. They are visualized as two blades of a pair of scissors, making it impossible to ascertain which one fixes the value of a product. The concept of marginal utility lies behind the demand curve, while the notion of sacrifice (i.e. cost of production) lies behind the supply curve. Marshall, therefore, brings the cost of production into view as a determinant of value.

2. CONSUMER SURPLUS: The concept of consumer surplus is derived from a demand curve as illustrated in figure 5. At point A on the demand curve the marginal utility of the fifth unit of good X is valued at $5.00; at point B the marginal utility of the eleventh unit is $3.00; and at point C the marginal utility of the fourteenth unit is $2.00. If the price is $2.00 per unit, those individuals with a marginal utility (i.e. satisfaction derived from a good X) greater than $2.00 will receive a surplus, indicated by the shaded area, because the monetary satisfaction they derive from the good is greater than its price. Although the idea of consumer surplus is abstract, Marshall was able to use it to demonstrate the effect of taxes on demand curves of different elasticities. And in this manner, Marshall tried to show what forms of government tax policy are desirable.

3. EQUILIBRIUM PERIODS: Marshall distinguished between four different equilibrium periods for supply and demand. They are as follows:

    (a) MARKET: The market equilibrium is the immediate situation where the supply of a product is fixed. Thus, a change in demand can only result in an increase in price without any immediate effect on supply.
    (b) SHORT RUN: In the short run, supply may be varied slightly by increasing the variable factors (i.e. labor, raw materials, etc.).
    (c) LONG RUN: In the long run, the fixed factors of production such as the firm's plant and machinery may be altered to meet changes in demand. In this case the supply curve will be very elastic, which will permit an expansion of output without a change in price.
    (d) EXTRA LONG RUN: In this length of time economic variables such as technology, tastes and population are subject to change.

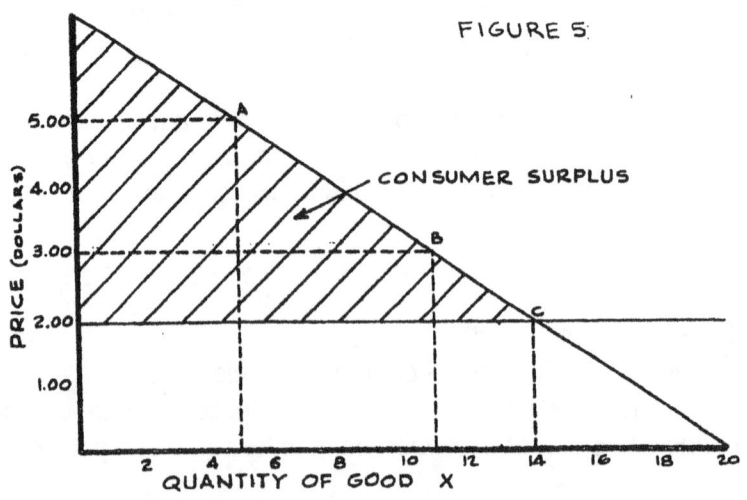

FIGURE 5

## JOHN MAYNARD KEYNES (1883-1946)

In 1919, Keynes, after having served as an advisor to the British government at Versailles, published the Economic Consequences of the Peace in which he attacked the Versailles Treaty. He regarded it as impractical and dangerous. On the one hand, it attempted to destroy Germany's economic system, Keynes argued, and on the other hand, it ordered Germany to pay an impossibly large reparation sum for war damage. Keynes correctly foresaw in the consequences of the treaty the resurgence of German nationalism and militarism. In the years following World War I, Keynes wrote A Tract on Monetary Reform (1923) and A Treatise on Money (1930), both of which are particularly concerned with the monetary mechanism and its relationship to economic fluctuations. These works, however, are overshadowed by The General Theory of Employment, Money and Interest (1936), a book which caused a revolution in economic thinking. Written in the time of the greatest depression of the modern era, the General Theory explained how the level of employment and income are determined; and most important, Keynes' theoretical analysis showed that full employment is not necessarily the equilibrium level of employment. In other words, there are no automatic forces existing to pull an economy out of a depression and restore full employment.